All-Terrain Pushchair Walks
Surrey

Published by Sigma Leisure – an imprint of Sigma Press, Stobart House, Pontyclerc, Penybanc Road, Ammanford, Carmarthenshire SA18 3HP.

British Library Cataloguing in Publication Data
A CIP record for this book is available from the British Library.

ISBN: 978-1-85058-906-8

Typesetting and Design by: Sigma Press, Ammanford, Carmarthenshire

Cover photograph: © Eleanor Simmons

Photographs: © Eleanor Simmons, Mark Breslin and Sabrina Droom

Printed by: TJ International Ltd, Padstow, Cornwall

Disclaimer: the information in this book is given in good faith and is believed to be correct at the time of publication. No responsibility is accepted by either the author or publisher for errors or omissions, or for any loss or injury howsoever caused. Only you can judge your own fitness, competence and experience. Do not rely solely on sketch maps for navigation: we strongly recommend the use of appropriate Ordnance Survey (or equivalent) maps.

All-Terrain Pushchair Walks Surrey

Eleanor Simmons

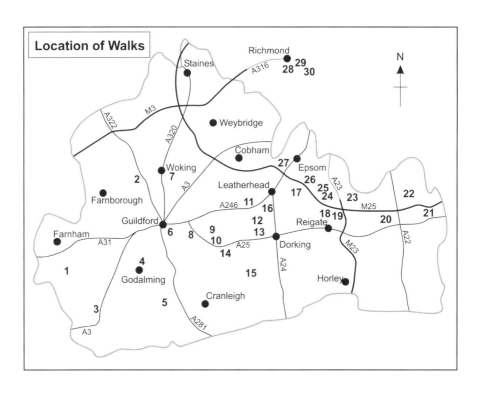

Location of Walks

Contents

The Walks

Introduction

This book aims to provide buggy walkers with a guide to a wide selection of routes that take in some of the highlights of the Surrey countryside. The walks vary from leisurely ambles along flat towpaths to lung busting hikes – perhaps not dissimilar from the kind of challenges you might have enjoyed pre-parenthood, only now, in addition to your backpack and OS map you will have a baby and all of their paraphernalia to accompany you!

Many of the walks are located in the Surrey Hills, an Area of Outstanding Natural Beauty, and take you to some of the county's most well known beauty spots –including Leith Hill and Devil's Punch Bowl. The landscape varies from grassland, open heath, chalk hills and woodland trails and is punctuated by picture perfect villages that provide refreshment to walkers in great country pubs and tea rooms.

The North Downs Way passes through the Surrey Hills and several walks take in sections of this 153 mile long distance path. Other trails that you will get to enjoy a taste of are the Greensand Way (a walk of 108 miles from Haslemere in Surrey to Hamstreet in Kent following the Greensand Ridge) and the Capital Ring (a 78 mile loop through the green spaces of London's suburbs).

There are hills aplenty but this is balanced by an equal number of low level walks including some along Surrey's waterways, taking in stretches of the River Thames, the Wey Navigations and Basingstoke Canal. If you prefer to get in the water rather than walk beside it, the Frensham Ponds walk starts and finishes at a beach! For London based walkers who don't want to roam too far from the capital, many walks are within the M25, including Richmond Park and Wimbledon Common.

Offering something for everyone, I hope this guide will enable you to explore new areas of the Surrey countryside or rediscover outdoor spaces you thought would be inaccessible with a buggy.

About this book

Each walk description begins with a summary of what you can expect from the route to help you choose one that suits your requirements. As well as information on the walk's landscape and points of interest, you will find details of the type of terrain, level of difficulty and length as well as any obstacles en route, e.g. stiles that make it suitable only when there are two people able to lift and carry the buggy.

Some walks have the option of short cuts or detours to points of interest – these are described to allow you to choose your preferred route. Opportunities for refreshments are also given including some of the fantastic pubs that the Surrey countryside has to offer.

Buggy passengers have not been forgotten in this guide! Many walks pass by farmland for animal spotting and ponds and rivers for duck feeding; these features are noted, as are any playgrounds and ice cream vans en route. Other child friendly attractions in the area are given to help you plan a fun filled day out.

Although each walk gives a suggested time required to complete it, this should only be taken as a guide. Toddlers who want to explore the countryside on foot rather than by buggy will obviously slow progress considerably as will breaks to appreciate the views, picnic, undertake nappy changes, etc, so make sure you give yourself plenty of time to complete and enjoy the walk.

Practical advice

Other than using a baby carrier, all terrain pushchairs (ATPs) are really the only way to get out walking in the countryside with your little one. They are capable of getting across tough terrain including mud, sand and snow and keep babies and children safe and comfortable over bumps.

A wide variety of models are currently on the market and share four key features that make them maneuverable in difficult terrain and safe and comfortable for passengers:

- Pneumatic tyres
- Long wheel base
- Lightweight frame
- Wheel suspension

When buying an ATP ensure it has these features as a minimum – remember that not all three wheelers are suited for all terrain. You will also need to consider other factors to inform your choice, such as size (will it fit in your car boot and through your front door); wheels (can the front wheel change from a fixed position to swivel, are the wheels quick release); baby accessories (can you fit a carry cot and/or car seat to it); handle bar (who will be pushing the buggy and can the handle bar be adjusted to their height) and cost (ATPs can be expensive in comparison with some other types of buggy but are often very well made and durable. Keep an eye out for sales or consider buying second hand.)

As a safety note, make sure that if you are walking with a very young baby that they are secure – remember that carry cots do not have a harness – and not being jolted over rough ground. Many of the walks are on flat even surfaces and it is a good idea to stick with these until your baby is a little older. If you are concerned by any tricky terrain you encounter, consider turning back or if there are two of you, lift the buggy over bumps.

Several routes in this book involve lifting the buggy over gates or stiles. While it would be preferable not to have this added challenge whilst out enjoying the countryside, in reality you cannot avoid these obstacles in many of the best areas for walking in Surrey. It would be a shame to be prevented from enjoying such beautiful countryside and luckily, so long as the obstacle is not too high, it is perfectly possible to carry the buggy over the top. We have managed to negotiate each gate and stile noted in this book. The photos on the following page show the steps needed to safely undertake this manoeuver. If you are worried, practice in advance or remove your child from the buggy and rest them on a blanket or ask a third person to hold them before attempting to lift your ATP.

What to take with you

This quick checklist provides a handy reference when deciding what to take with you when out walking. Make sure you take into consideration the weather conditions and how long you anticipate being outdoors. Think about how you want to carry everything. My preference is for a backpack that can be carried when you want to keep the buggy as light as possible and squeezed into the storage area under the buggy when buggy weight is not an issue.

Weather protection: rain cover, sun cover, sleeping bag/foot muff.

Suggested way of negotiating a gate or stile

Milk: for bottle fed babies, formula can most easily be carried in ready to use cartons or a powder dispenser, which you can mix with water when needed. If your baby only takes warm milk, carry a flask of hot water with you.

Refreshments: picnic and/or snacks and drinks for adults and children. Handy snacks include breadsticks, rice cakes and raisins. You might want to avoid food pots that are not re-sealable if your child is unlikely to eat all of it, as it can get messy to transport half eaten yogurts!

Changing equipment: nappies, wipes and nappy bags.

Clothing: dress your little one in clothes and head gear appropriate for the weather but bear in mind that conditions might change so being able to add or remove layers is important. Remember that buggy passengers will not be working up a sweat as you may be, so even if you are peeling off your hat and coat, babies might still be chilly – keep a check of their temperature. If toddlers want to get out of their buggy they will need appropriate shoes or wellies.

Entertainment: a few toys or board books that can be attached to the buggy are a good idea if being in the great outdoors is not satisfactory entertainment for your little one.

Safety: mobile phone, first aid kit, sun cream, puncture repair kit, tyre pump, Ordnance Survey map, this guide book!

The Countryside Code

The Countryside Code is dedicated to helping members of the public respect, protect and enjoy the countryside:

- Be safe, plan ahead and follow any signs
- Leave gates and property as you find them
- Protect plants and animals and take your litter home
- Keep dogs under close control
- Consider other people

For more information go to **www.naturalengland.org.uk**

Key to symbols

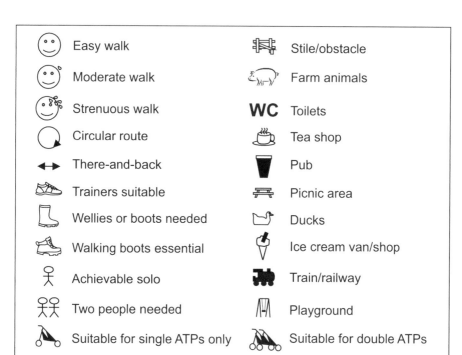

☺	Easy walk	Stile/obstacle
☺	Moderate walk	Farm animals
☺	Strenuous walk	**WC** Toilets
	Circular route	Tea shop
↔	There-and-back	Pub
	Trainers suitable	Picnic area
	Wellies or boots needed	Ducks
	Walking boots essential	Ice cream van/shop
	Achievable solo	Train/railway
	Two people needed	Playground
	Suitable for single ATPs only	Suitable for double ATPs

Walk 1
Frensham Ponds

Make sure you bring your bucket and spade and swim wear for this walk! It starts and finishes at Frensham Great Pond's sandy beach where you can enjoy a paddle or a swim and of course build sandcastles.

The route takes you to both of Frensham's ponds, through the heathland of Frensham Common that separates them and includes a climb to a ridgeway with fine views on either side towards the two ponds. The ponds are man-made, created in the Middle Ages to provide fish for the Bishop of Winchester's estate. During the Second World War the ponds were drained in an attempt to make the landscape unidentifiable and the land used as a training ground by Canadian troops.

Most of the walk is on good footpaths and bridleways but several sections are on sand. All terrain buggies handle sand well though the lighter the passenger the easier progress will be! For a shorter stroll, it is possible to do circular walks of either pond – it is a one mile lap of Little Pond or 1.5 miles around Great Pond, though neither avoids having to contend with the sandy surface. The attraction of an inland beach make Frensham a busy spot on a summer weekend but during

Distance	4 miles
Allow	2 hours
Map	OS 1:25000 Explorer 145. Grid reference SU845400
Getting there	Parking is available at the start of the walk on Bacon Lane just off the A287 between Hindhead and Farnham. Parking is free

the week and you will find that it returns to its natural tranquillity. Toilets, baby changing facilities and a snack bar with outdoor seating are all to be found at Great Pond.

1. Facing the pond with the information centre behind you, take the sandy track to the left between two wooden fences and when you reach the summit of this short incline continue ahead on the grass past a small silver birch tree. You soon reach an open sandy area with a view of the pond to the right and the road ahead. Take the left hand fork down the sandy slope.

2. At the bottom of the slope, cross over the road by the bus stop and continue through the heather filled open heathland. The terrain here is less sandy. You will see a hill ahead of you which you should climb via the right hand track and then descend straight down the slope on the opposite side of the summit.

At the summit is a Bronze Age burial ground and hundreds of Bronze Age arrowheads have been found in the area.

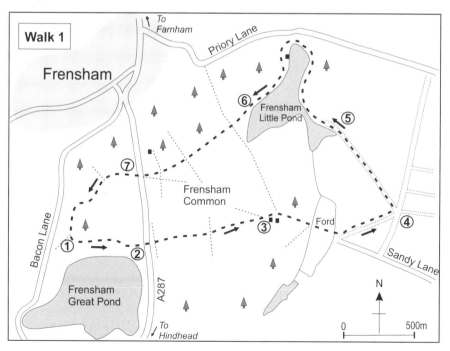

3. At the bottom of the hill turn left and push the buggy under the red and white barrier. Turn right past the cottages and along the surfaced byway (Sandy Lane), crossing the bridge over the ford. 100 metres past the ford, fork left away from the lane onto the signposted bridleway. There is a footpath that runs alongside the bridleway which makes for an easier passage through the coniferous woodland.

4. After 400 metres you reach a junction, turn left onto the footpath, keeping the paddock to your right. This shaded path will take you past a large pine tree plantation and eventually comes out by a

Through the woodland of Frensham Common

National Trust sign for Frensham Little Pond. Continue straight ahead keeping the fence to your right. The pond itself soon comes into view to the left of the path.

Frensham Little Pond is a haven for wildlife and no swimming or water sports are permitted.

5. Follow the wide flat trail around the pond anticlockwise. After crossing a footbridge by the dam the path follows the roadside for a short time. When you see an orange National Trust arrow on a signpost bear left gently uphill towards woodland. This will return you to the pond's shoreline.

6. Follow the shoreline until you reach a sandy junction where six paths converge. Take the second path on the left which heads gently uphill to a bench at the summit. From this high ridge you can look back down at Little Pond and if you cross the bridleway

to the other side of the ridge a second bench provides a rest point with a view towards Great Pond. Head down the steep grassy slope by the bench and through the scrub at the bottom. When you meet with a sandy track head along it towards the gate by the roadside.

7. Cross over the road and follow the wide sandy bridleway back to the car park. It makes for quite a challenging end to the walk but look out for a boardwalk to the left of the bridleway for an easier last few hundred metres.

Walk 2
Basingstoke Canal

If you're looking for a fun, easy to navigate walk then this is the one for you as there is heaps to see and the canal towpath does all the route finding for you! It takes in six of the Basingstoke Canal's thirty two miles and has been included as a point to point walk, starting and finishing at different train stations, but if you prefer you can easily enjoy a shorter section of the canal and then return the same way for an out and back trip. A four mile round trip to Guildford Road Bridge would allow you to take in Mytchett Lake, the canal visitor centre and Frimley Lodge Park with its miniature railway and playgrounds. Continuing further will take you through the tranquil stretch of the canal through Deepcut and passes a series of locks in pretty woodland. The land adjacent to much of this walk is owned by the Ministry of Defence, but apart from the occasional sound of rifle fire you would hardly know it!

Distance	6 miles (but shorter variations possible)
Allow	3-4 hours
Map	OS 1:25000 Explorer 145. Grid reference SU892533
Getting there	The walk starts from Ash Vale station on the line between London Waterloo and Farnham. If you have arrived by train, exit onto Station Approach (not the main exit from the station) via a lengthy series of steps. Car users can park at the top of Station Approach for £1 on weekdays or for free at weekends

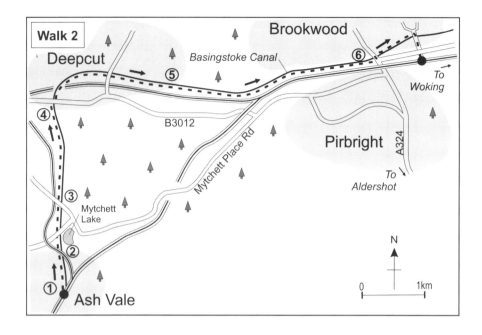

The visitor centre has a café, picnic area and toilets. You could also stop for refreshment half way along the route at the Kings Head at Guildford Bridge Road or the Brookwood Hotel at the end of the walk.

1. From the station, turn left up Station Approach to meet with the canal at the top. Turn left onto the tow path, under the railway bridge.

   You will more than likely find a team of ducks paddling over to greet you but don't feed them all your bread as there are ducks, swans and geese dotted along the whole route!

2. You soon go past the peaceful expanse of Mytchett Lake and after about a mile reach the canal visitor centre that can be accessed by crossing the swing bridge over the canal.

   The visitor centre has a museum, café, picnic tables and a play area and in the summer months and school holidays, if you don't fancy walking any further, there are boat trips starting from here.

3. Return back across the bridge to the towpath and continue onwards to Frimley Lodge Park.

If you happen to be doing this walk on the first Sunday of the month, your first indication that you have reached the park will probably be seeing or hearing the miniature trains that are operated on this day. As well as taking a ride on the train you might want to enjoy the other activities and facilities this large open space has to offer: a brand new playground, pitch and putt course, picnic and bbq area and café.

4. At the perimeter of the park, you reach Guildford Road Bridge which you should cross to rejoin the towpath on the opposite side of the canal, which soon bears round to the right.

Just past the attractive gatehouse lodge after Guildford Road Bridge you will find yourself on the easily missed Frimley aqueduct – look to your left to see the railway line below.

Half a mile further on you pass under Deepcut Bridge and enter a mile long stretch of peaceful canal flanked on either side by a steep embankment.

5. After reaching the first of 14 locks the 'deep cut' ends and the route opens into pretty woodland, which continues for a very attractive and tranquil two mile stretch. The path also improves greatly from this point.

6. When you reach Pirbright Bridge cross over and rejoin the tow path on the north side of

The walk passes pretty woodland along the towpath

the canal, continuing until the green metal bridge which returns you back to the opposite side. Head straight up, crossing the main road to reach Brookwood Station.

Walk 3
Devil's Punch Bowl

This route takes in fine views from the top of this natural amphitheatre as well as the quiet, pretty woodland within the bowl. With such contrasting atmospheres it almost feels like two walks in one. You are likely to see Exmoor ponies grazing by the paths at the top of the bowl and hear the sound of woodpeckers in the trees of the lower woodland. It is also home to rare bird species including the Dartford warbler, nightjar and woodlark. The route also passes close by the attractive 18th century Keeper's Cottage which is worth the short detour to admire.

The terrain is mostly good for buggy walking with wide tracks, although a short stretch within the bowl can be very bumpy and rutted as it is used by farm vehicles and so depending on conditions it may be easier to carry the buggy for a few metres. A fairly steep descent into the bowl, and a lengthy ascent back up merit this route a difficult rating. You will also need to lift the buggy over two fairly high farm gates where the kissing gates intended for walkers are too narrow to squeeze through. For an easy, flat walk you could just take a 1.5 mile round trip to the Robertson memorial.

Distance	3 miles
Allow	1.5 hours
Map	OS 1:25000 Explorer 133. Grid reference SU 891357
Getting there	The walk starts from the National Trust Devil's Punch Bowl car park in Hindhead which is signposted from the A3. There is a fee for parking

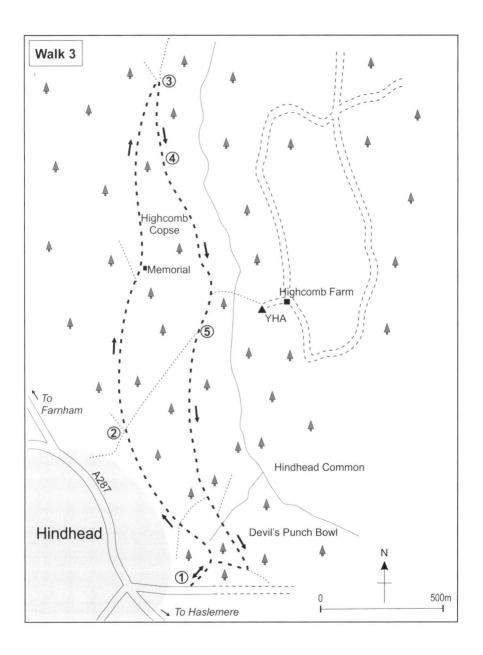

Walk 3

To Farnham

Highcomb Copse

Memorial

Highcomb Farm

YHA

Hindhead

Hindhead Common

Devil's Punch Bowl

To Haslemere

N

0   500m

1. From the car park head to the view point for your first look down into the basin and from here turn left onto the wide path that heads into woodland. Continue through the woods until you reach Highcombe Edge car park from where several tracks head off in different directions. Take the route that passes through a gate by an information board.

   You are now out of the dense woodland and onto heath with views across Devil's Punch Bowl.

2. Continue ahead on the wide open track and when you reach a three way junction after 500 metres, take the right hand fork.

   You will see a water trough a short way down the left path making this a likely location to spot grazing ponies.

   This short detour off the main track takes you to the Robertson memorial where a bench makes this a pleasant spot to relax and enjoy the views. The path continues along the top of the basin and then slowly begins to descend across the heathland. If you want to avoid descending into the basin, you can retrace your steps to the car park from the memorial.

3. Half a mile from the memorial the path forks as it re-enters woodland, take the right hand track and then almost immediately turn sharp right down a fairly steep sunken path. Enclosed by holly on each bank it feels magical to leave the open space at the top of the basin and descend into its depths.

4. At the bottom of the hill you'll see the 18th century Keeper's Cottage to the left. It is worth taking the short detour for a closer look and then returning to the route which continues straight ahead with farmland to your left and woods to the right. Pass through the open gate and continue alongside the row of beech trees that form the old hedgebank boundary.

   You are now on Sailor's Lane which can become quiet rough terrain if it has been heavily used by farm vehicles. There may be short stretches where it is easier for two people to carry the buggy but it is not long before you return to a better path. Further along the lane

The ATP coping well with the snowy conditions at Devil's Punch Bowl

you can see and hear Smallbrook stream lower down the basin to your left.

5. Ignore the path that heads uphill to your right and continue ahead on the track that is signposted 'Pedestrian path, no horses or cyclists'. After lifting the buggy over a gate (the kissing gate next to it is too narrow to pass through) slowly meander along the woodland path that rises back up the side of the basin, gently at first and then steeper as you get higher. It is a very pretty stretch of the walk, with beech trees rising high above you, that makes for highly enjoyable walking in spite of the tiring ascent. Upon reaching the summit, turn right and lift the buggy over another gate to return to the car park.

Walk 4 Godalming to Guildford on the Wey Navigation

This route offers easy walking along a five mile stretch of the River Wey Navigation. You will pass locks, colourful moored barges and grazing cattle as you walk through the meadows and woodland of the towpath. The only potential difficulty en route is likely to be mud if there has been rain.

The walk is described as a point-to-point route starting in Godalming and ending in Guildford (using the train as your sole form of transport or as a means of returning to your car) but you could reverse it without any difficulty or undertake a shorter stretch as an out and back route. There are pubs, cafés and shops aplenty in Godalming and Guildford as well as The Parrot Inn at Broadford Bridge around the halfway point of the route.

Distance	5 miles
Allow	3 hours
Map	OS 1:25 000 Explorer 145. Grid reference SU996439
Getting there	The walk starts from Godalming Station on the line between London Waterloo and Portsmouth. If you have arrived by train, exit onto Station Approach. Car users can park at the station or at one of the car parks in the town

1. Turn left out of the station and head down Station Approach. With St Peter and St Paul's Church in front of you, turn left and enter Phillips Memorial Ground (where you will find a children's playground).

Look out for the Philips Memorial Cloister built in 1913 to commemorate Jack Phillips, Chief Wireless Telegraphist on the Titanic who remained at his post, as the ship sank on 15 April 1912, while signalling for help using the new international emergency call sign SOS.

2. Follow the tarmac path which meanders alongside the River Wey. When you reach Town Bridge, cross the road and rejoin the towpath which is a little narrow in places. The area on the opposite side of the river is known as Lammas Land and you are likely to see cattle grazing in the meadow. After Catteshall Lock the towpath switches to the opposite bank of the river on a wider path and the environment soon feels more tranquil as you leave the town behind you and walk through woodland and meadows.

Catteshall Lock is next to Farncombe Boat House with lots of moored barges. The Boat House also has a café if you want to take an early break.

Taking a break at St Catherine's lock

3. After crossing over the small road bridge by Tiltham's Farm the towpath is uninterrupted as you walk past Unstead Lock and through Peasmarsh to reach Broadford Bridge. Cross the busy road bridge to rejoin the towpath.

4. Half a mile beyond the bridge you reach St Catherine's Lock. The land is National Trust owned and is home to grazing Highland cattle. If you

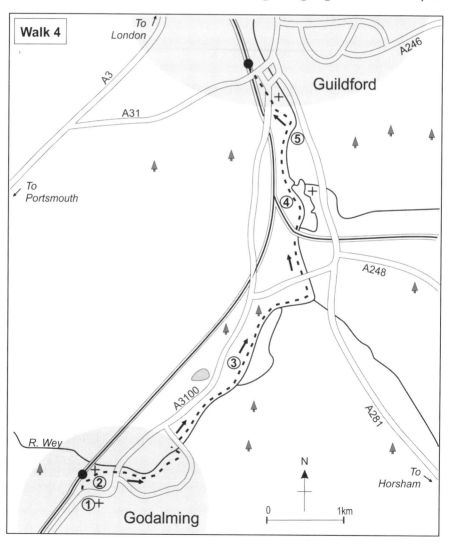

are lucky enough to pass at the same time as a barge is negotiating the lock, it is a lovely place to stop and take a break. The stretch of river beyond the lock is very pretty as the waterway winds its way through woodland.

5. Half a mile outside of Guildford the castle comes into view and the riverbank is lined with beautiful willow trees. At the weir just before Guildford Rowing Club, turn left where you will find a pleasant grassy area, home to moored boats and ducks, making it a fun picnic spot. When you reach Millmead Lock go left at the bridge and continue along the waterside. After passing under the road bridge head up the walkway to the main road and follow signs to the station.

Walk 5
Hascombe Hill

Starting from the attractive village of Hascombe this walk takes you high onto Hascombe Hill with fine views of the surrounding countryside and light aircraft using nearby Dunsfold Aerodrome.

Although the majority of the tracks used for this route are wide, some can be very muddy and bumpy so bear in mind recent weather conditions when embarking on this walk. One stretch is probably more easily tackled by carrying the buggy unless you and the buggy occupant are competent and happy at getting across very bumpy terrain.

The White Horse pub makes for a great finishing point. It serves good food, has a large garden and a toy box! It was previously the 'local' for film star Dirk Bogarde and more recently television presenter and radio broadcaster Chris Evans. Alternatively the village pond is a lovely spot for a picnic and feeding the ducks.

Distance	2.5 miles
Allow	2 hours
Map	1:25000 Explorer 134. Grid reference TQ001394
Getting there	The walk starts from the car park opposite the White Horse pub in Hascombe on the B2130, five miles south of Godalming. Parking is free

1. Head up the tarmac Nore Lane immediately right of pub which rises gently uphill. After 100m you reach Hascombe Place farmhouse. Turn right on footpath that goes behind a garage. The path is marked by a

yellow arrow and widens to form a sunken path going uphill. Follow the path as it bears left, continuing uphill. It is a steep ascent but as you near the top there are lovely views to the right down and across the valley.

2. The path forks and you need to bear right onto the lower track which soon levels out and the fine views continue. When you reach a T-junction by rhododendron bushes and a large beech tree, turn right. This high level track curves anticlockwise around the hill. When you reach a log seat on a sandy bank take a break to enjoy the view of the Wey Navigation through a large gap in the trees.

Just in front of the Wey is Dunsfold Aerodrome. It was built and used by the Canadian Airforce in World War Two. It is now used as the location for filming the television show Top Gear but you are still likely to see aircraft taking off and coming into land.

3. After 400 metres the path forks and the main track heads downhill. Ignore this major track and bear left on a rising path. Pass a metal fence and go under the holly tree that arches over the track to begin

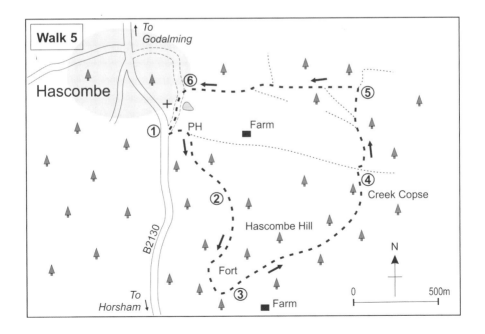

the descent back down Hascombe Hill. The path starts gently but steepens as you get closer to the valley floor.

4. When you reach the bottom go round a wooden fence and turn right onto the sunken bridleway for 20 metres before turning left onto wide path heading uphill. The path levels and there are views of the fields of Hascombe Place Farm to your left. Continue straight ahead and when the path forks, ignore the left hand path marked with a blue arrow and bear right.

5. Turn sharp left when you reach a junction by the corner of the hill onto a broad but potentially muddy and bumpy track. Continue to descend, ignoring several intersecting bridleways. The final stretch is quite tricky and it may be easier to carry the buggy.

6. When you emerge onto the tarmac follow the quiet road past the village pond, St Peter's Church and several attractive cottages. Soon after you will see the White Horse pub and car park ahead.

Checking the route back to the White Horse pub

Walk 6
St Martha's Church

A beautiful walk at any time of the year, but if you can time your trip here to coincide with the bluebell season then you are in for a real treat as Chantry Wood bursts into colour amid a carpet of this beautiful wild flower. Whatever the season, this out and back walk to St Martha's Church provides great views towards Newlands Corner from this spectacularly located church on the North Downs Way.

The route includes two strenuous uphills and reciprocal descents on the return journey, as well as a stretch through sand which is challenging to push a buggy (and probably easier to carry if there are two of you). Aside from these obstacles the route follows good, wide paths that present few difficulties.

Distance	3.5 miles
Allow	2 hours
Map	OS 1:25000 Explorer 146. Grid reference TQ00384834
Getting there	The walk starts from Pilgrims Way car park which is half way between Guildford and Shalford on the A281 (Shalford Road). Parking is free. If travelling by public transport, both Shalford and Guildford stations are about a mile away

1. From the car park, take the track by Chantry Cottage that heads gradually uphill. To your right is Chantry Wood and views of rolling farmland, with horses grazing in the fields to the left..

2. After about ½ mile on this wide track the surface suddenly becomes sandy as you cross through a field. It is challenging terrain with a pushchair and you may find it easier to pull rather than push the buggy. Luckily this section of the route only lasts for 200 metres and then returns to a decent track upon entering woodland. The path immediately splits – continue straight ahead ascending through Chantry Wood on this undulating stretch of the North Downs Way.

3. The track meets with a road after ¼ mile, turn left onto Halfpenny Way for 30 metres before taking the path to the right after Southernway Cottage. Continue on this path for ½ mile to reach St Martha's Church on the steep track.

4. When you reach the summit head to the southern side of the church to recover on one of the many benches while enjoying the fabulous view of the Surrey Hills. When you're ready, retrace your steps to the entry to Chantry Wood on Halfpenny Lane

   The church dates back to the 12th century and is only accessible by foot giving it a special, secluded feel.

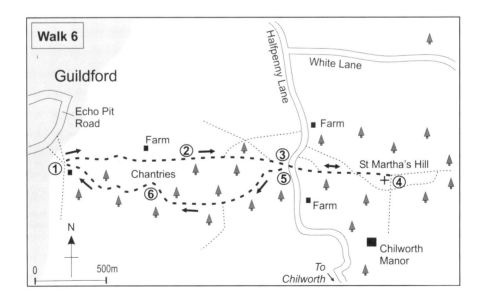

Enjoying the views from St Martha's Church

5. Instead of returning back down the North Downs Way, bear left into the woods. After 200 metres the path splits three ways, take the middle route which bears around the southern perimeter of the woods with fine views to the left of the Weald. Shortly after you pass a bench by a stile, bear left when the path forks and continue onwards ignoring all intersecting paths.

6. Eventually, the track bears right and meets with a junction. Turn left onto this wide track that is signposted 'Scholars Trail'. The wood opens out and the path passes through a grassy area before re-entering the woods to descend on the Scholars Trail back to Chantry Cottage and the start of the route.

Walk 7
Ripley Green and the Wey Navigation

Starting at Ripley Green, this route takes in a variety of landscapes and some interesting sights as it passes Ockham Mill and meanders along a section of the River Wey Navigation. You will see plenty of colourful barges along the Wey, either moored or navigating the canal and there are opportunities in abundance to feed the ducks.

The paths are generally good but a little uneven in places. It is included as a two person walk as there is a stile crossing and a steep footbridge where it may be easier to carry the buggy.

The Anchor Pub at Pyrford Lock serves good food and has outdoor seating by the canal in summer and a log fire inside for the winter. Various shops and pubs can be found in Ripley and there is a picnic area and playground on Ripley Green..

Distance	2 miles, or 3 if you want to extend it to Pyrford Lock for refreshments
Allow	2 hours
Map	OS 1:250000 Explorer 145. Grid reference TQ053571
Getting there	The walk starts from the Dunsborough Park car park at Ripley Green to the north east of Ripley Village off the B2215. Parking is free. Ripley village is accessible by bus (562) from Woking and from there it is just a short walk to the start

1. At the far end of the car park, cross over the road and go round the low barrier onto the green where three paths head off in different directions. Take the path furthest left and head diagonally across the grass. Ignore the footpath sign heading into the woods after 300 metres and continue straight on. When you meet a second fork in the path after a further 100 metres, take the right hand path into woodland, which shortly crosses a wooden bridge over a stream. You now find yourself on a pretty tree lined bridleway which crosses a second footbridge before meeting with Mill Lane.

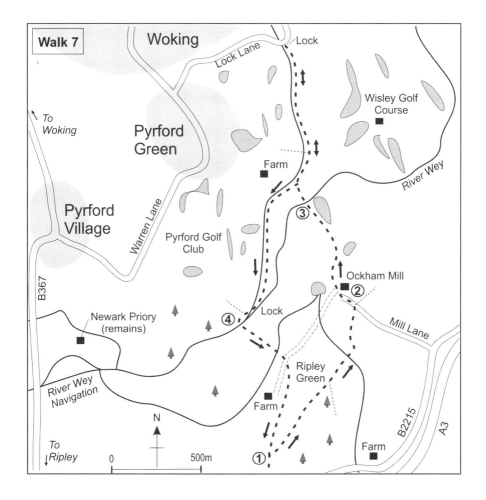

2. Turn left onto the lane and go through the gate signposted 'private' (the footpath sign is just to the left of the gate) and before you is the impressive and unusual Ockham Mill. The lane bears right after the mill and you cross a low stile to continue along a pleasant footpath.

The mill dates back to 1862 though it stopped working in 1927 and lay disused until 1958. Since then the mill has been used as a private residence.

3. 400 metres beyond the mill you cross a footbridge high over the River Wey and shortly after reach the tow path of the Wey Navigation. If you want to see a longer stretch of the canal and take a break at the Anchor Pub at Pyrford Lock turn right. When sufficiently refreshed, you will have to retrace your steps to this point. If you are not taking the detour to Pyrford Lock, turn left and follow the towpath until Walsham Gates.

En route to Walsham Gates you will pass Pyrford Place on the opposite side, although the current building is 20th century housing private

The Wey Navigation towpath

apartments. The summerhouse right on the bank dates to the 17th century.

4. At Walsham Gates, pass the cottage and then cross the River Wey at the weir. Continue straight ahead on the footpath beyond the weir that goes between two fields. Turn right when you reach the attractive River End Cottage and go up the lane, bearing right at the top to return to the car park.

Walk 8
Newlands Corner

Located on the North Downs Way, this short walk starting from Newlands Corner has great views of the Surrey Hills looking down to the village of Albury. Spring and summer bring a carpet of wildflowers to the slopes, while the visitor centre at Newlands Corner has some interesting exhibits and activities for children.

The route follows mostly grassy tracks on the slopes of the downs but it's a short enough walk for the uphill stretches to not be overly challenging. Frequent stops to take in the views will also provide the perfect distraction from aching calf muscles!

Drinks and snacks are available from the kiosk in the car park with outdoor seating. In chilly weather, The Barn coffee shop on the opposite side of the A25 is a warmer option offering a full menu – just take care when crossing the busy road.

Distance	1 mile
Allow	45 minutes
Map	1:250000 Explorer 145. Grid reference TQ042492
Getting there	The walk starts from Newlands Corner car park on the A25 north west of Shere. Parking is free

1. With your back to the visitor centre, cross the car park and onto the grassy slope in front of you. Head along the rough track that leads diagonally right into a small wooded area. You quickly exit the trees

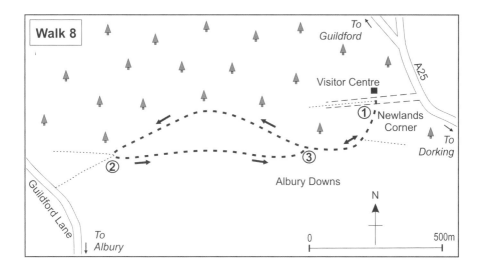

The Downs at Newlands Corner

and should then follow the track that hugs the woodland to your right. The track itself soon peters out but remain on the grass, keeping the woods to your right, ignoring any paths that head into the trees.

2. Follow the slope downhill until a way marker points right for the North Downs Way. Here you turn left back across the middle of the slope on the grassy path, which joins with the original track after 500 metres.

3. Retrace your steps through the wooded area and up the hill to return to the car park.

Walk 9
Francis Corner

This easy walk through the woods at Netley Heath follows wide flat paths and takes in a section of the Norths Down Way. If your children are walking it's a great autumn stroll for kicking through the leaves and for adults, this route could be used to burn a few calories after enjoying Sunday lunch in one of the great country pubs in nearby Shere. A pretty stream runs through the village which is home to a wealth of noisy ducks who love to be fed, so make sure you arrive armed with bread.

Distance	2 miles
Allow	1 hour
Map	OS 1:25 000 Explorer 145. Grid reference TQ078496
Getting there	Parking is available at the start of the walk on Coombe Lane which runs between East Horsley and Shere. The car park is not shown on OS maps but if driving from Shere it is on the right hand side about a mile and a half after you turn off the A25. There is a signpost for the car park but it is a little tucked away. Parking is free

Fun in the fallen autumn leaves

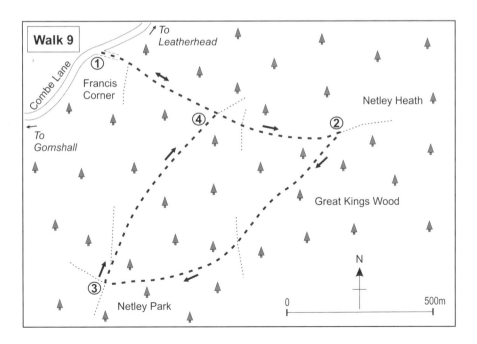

1. From the car park head into the woods on the wide track marked 'Easy Access Route'. After 100 metres go round the barrier and continue past the pine trees. Upon reaching a major junction, take the path diagonally across.

2. After 300 metres, when the path intersects with a wide track, turn right, which although not signposted is the North Downs Way. Ignore any turn offs until you reach a barrier at the Netley Plantation.

3. Turn right at the barrier and at a fork after 50 metres, continue straight ahead, going around another barrier.

4. After a further 600 metres, turn left when you reach a junction to return to the car park.

Walk 10
Abinger Roughs and Hackhurst Downs

For buggy walkers who relish a challenge, this is a tough, lengthy route that provides great rewards for the effort put in. It takes you through the attractive woodland of Abinger Roughs and Broomy Downs, but the real highlight is the ascent to the North Downs Way with amazing views towards Ranmore Common. Once you are on the traverse across the North Downs Way the views back down into the valley from which you ascended will leave you impressed at how high you have climbed.

The terrain is variable, from wide bridleways and surfaced byways enabling easy walking to more demanding footpaths which may be

Distance	**6 miles (or 7 miles if taking detour to Gomshall)**
Allow	**3-4 hours**
Map	**1:25000 Explorer 145 and 146.** **Grid reference TQ111480**
Getting there	**The walk starts from the Abinger Rough car park at the southern end of Whitedown Lane just off the Dorking Road (A25) between Abinger Hammer and Wooton. If travelling by public transport, you will need to walk from Gomshall Station to the footpath described at point 7 of the walk – there is a pavement alongside the A25 from the station but you will need to cross to the opposite side of the road. This will add a total of 1 mile to the route**

narrow, rocky, strewn with exposed tree roots or present all three obstacles at once! Aside from the sustained uphill stretch to reach the North Downs Way, it is a fairly undulating route so a good level of fitness is essential. There are also four gates which require lifting the buggy over.

Given the length of the walk taking some provisions with you is advisable and there several benches and grassy areas along the North Downs Way to enjoy a picnic with a view. Alternatively, you could take a detour into Gomshall for a great country pub lunch at The Gomshall Mill Inn or tea and cake at the village's café. Both are very family friendly and the pub has a play area in the garden and stream running through it, complete with a bridge for a game of Pooh sticks.

1. From the car park go through a gate at the far end and along the grassy path which gradually descends and passes a large tree on the left that older children love to climb thanks to its low branches. Very shortly after passing the tree turn sharply right back on yourself. The bridleway hugs the field on the left and keeps woodland on the right. You'll pass by a monument to Samuel Wilberforce opposite Leasers Barn and its flock of sheep.

   The monument marks the spot Bishop Samuel Wilberforce, son of William Wilberforce, fell from his horse and died in 1873.

2. When you reach the road, cross carefully and continue along the bridleway opposite where there is a sign for the National Cycle Network. The track is fenced between farmland and Deerleap Wood and it is here that you gain the first views ahead towards Ranmore Common. After passing Park Farm turn left away from the cycle route and onto another bridleway that will take you across a railway bridge. You are now on a farm track that will potentially be very muddy. Walk towards the woods ahead of you and through a gate.

3. Once in the woods, the ascent towards the North Downs Way begins! Ignore the path immediately to the right and head uphill on the trail signposted with a blue arrow which immediately starts to bear steeply around to the right. You soon reach a fork – continue uphill

   The rough terrain and steepness make for a challenging climb but there are numerous breaks in the trees to reveal the views eastwards

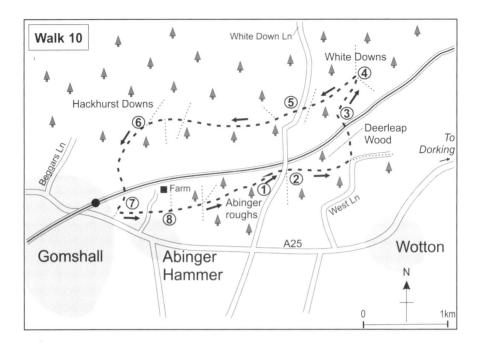

to Dorking and Ranmore, including the spire of St Barnabas Church, commonly known as 'The Church on the North Downs Way'.

After about 400 metres of uphill climbing the view is accompanied by a bench for you to take a break and fully enjoy the panorama. Soon after you reach a metal gate which signifies the end of the climb.

To the right of the metal gate you will see a brick built pill box. It is the first of several that you will pass along the North Downs Way. Built in 1940, they form part of a network of defences manned by the Home Guard to protect London from German invasion.

4. Turn left just before the metal gate to begin the stretch of the walk along the North Downs Way. The NDW is well signposted, making navigation easy but the terrain in places can be difficult. Some stretches are narrow and can by rough and bumpy underfoot so care is needed and progress may be a little slow. Nonetheless, there are great views back down to the route you have taken. After 400 metres

on the NDW you reach a kissing gate that you will need to lift the buggy over.

5. Cross Whitedown Lane after a further 400 metres and rejoin the NDW on the opposite side of the road. The path heads steeply uphill for 50 metres and then bears left, passing through a gate at White Downs Lease. The grassy area and benches at Blatchford Down are a pleasant spot for a picnic and will allow you to gather your strength for three more buggy lifts over kissing gates. The first two, immediately next to the grassy area where a bridleway cuts through the NDW and then the third a little further on after descending a gentle grassy slope.

6. When you reach the public byway, turn left and head downhill on this steep but surfaced lane. Make sure you listen out for motorcycles as it's a popular route for off-road bikes. The byway leads all the way to the A25 – if you are taking a detour into Gomshall, descend all the way to the road and carefully cross over to the pavement on the opposite side. Turn right for a ½ mile walk into the village and return by the same way.

7. If you are returning to the car park, turn left along a signposted footpath 200 metres before the road on a narrow track into woodland. After 200 metres along the footpath, go through a wooden gate and continue alongside a field where you can see Hackhurst Farm to your left and a view back up towards the NDW. Go through another gate at the end of the field, cross the road and continue on the bridleway opposite which is part of the National Cycle Network. This is good news as it means the remainder of the route is on easy buggy terrain.

A beautiful start to this challenging route at Abinger Roughs

49

8. Follow the wide gravel track up into woodland and continue straight ahead until you reach a grassy clearing. Ignore the paths heading off to the right and remain on the main track that bears gently left and heads gradually downhill. When it forks, head right to return to the car park.

Walk 11
Bookham Common

This route provides a pleasant stroll through the tranquil woods of Bookham Common. It passes a series of ponds rich in wildlife where various hides give you the chance to quietly observe the birdlife and waterfowl.

The terrain is entirely wide flat paths making for trouble free walking and older children could easily accompany walkers on their bicycles. There are no amenities en route but nearby Bookham has cafés, pubs and shops.

Distance	**1.25 miles**
Allow	**45 minutes**
Map	**OS 1:25000 Explorer 146. Grid reference TQ129556**
Getting there	**The walk starts from the National Trust's Tunnel car park just outside Bookham village. There is a fee for parking (free for NT members). If you are travelling by train, Bookham station is a few minutes walk away from the start of the walk**

1. From the car park take the path adjacent to the information board. When it forks after only 20 metres bear left where the signpost reads 'Vehicles to Handleys and Merritts cottage only'. The wide path heads through the oak trees and past Isle of Wight (I.O.W.) pond.

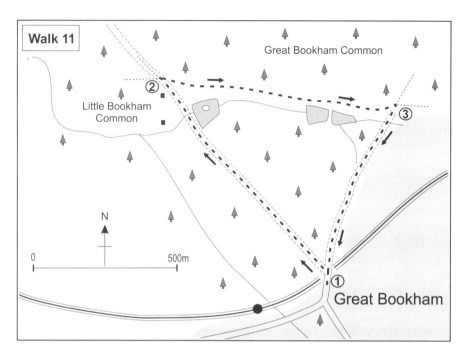

Walk 11

Great Bookham Common

Little Bookham Common

N

0   500m

Great Bookham

Peeping through one of the bird hides

2. When you reach Merritts Cottage bear right at the junction along a bridleway signposted to Fetcham. You will pass by several ponds, some of which have bird hides to allow you to get a closer look at the wildlife.

3. Soon after passing the last of the ponds you reach a junction where you can see houses ahead. Turn right here and go past a paddock on the left to return to the car park.

Peaceful pond at Bookham Common

Walk 12
Polesden Lacey

Polesden Lacey is a beautiful country house and gardens set in the Surrey Hills. The walk takes you along some of the estate's many paths and onto Ranmore Common, through woods and farmland with superb views of the house and the surrounding countryside.

The terrain is generally well suited for buggies with just a few potentially muddy stretches along bridleways and a number of hills to get the heart pumping. If you enjoy this walk, there are numerous other walking options within the estate for you to explore on another trip.

Should you wish to visit Polesden Lacey itself, the grounds are open all year round while the house has limited opening during the winter months; so if you are interested in venturing inside, make sure you check beforehand. The grounds include a woodland play area although it is better suited to older children. The café serves children's meals, has a microwave for warming milk and food and a selection of toys and books to keep youngsters occupied. On site there is also a toy shop packed with beautiful wooden toys and books!

Distance	3.5 miles
Allow	2.5 hours
Map	OS 1:25000 Explorer 146. Grid reference TQ135523
Getting there	Polesden Lacey is located off the A246 between Effingham and Leatherhead and is very well signposted. The walk starts from the National Trust car park. There is a fee for parking (free for NT members)

1. With the entrance to Polesden Lacey behind you, turn right along the roadside. As the road bears left, pass through the kissing gate which is wide enough for buggies. Walk straight ahead and then bear right, keeping the fence to your right, towards a wooden gate. Go through the gate and then cross a path to pass through a large kissing gate into another field. Keep the trees to your left to reach another gate that takes you into woodland.

2. Once through the gate, turn right along a sunken bridleway (Connicut Lane) which takes you downhill through Freehold Wood. This section of the route is potentially muddy. The path and surrounding trees are

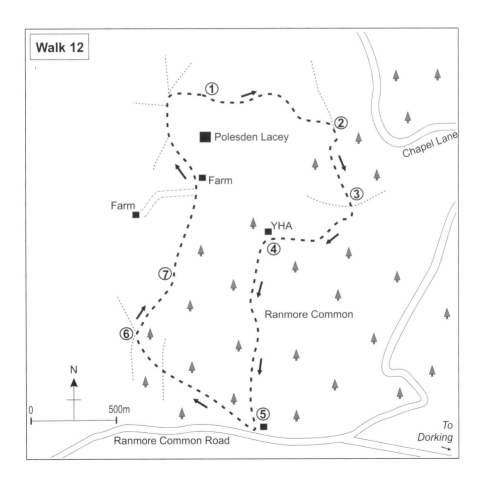

very pretty and you soon pass under the Italianate Bridge. Continue down the sunken path to reach the bottom of the hill.

3. Bear right at the bottom of the hill to continue along the sunken path, ignoring the path to the left. Look to your right for views of the Polesden Lacey gardens. The path climbs steadily until you reach Tanners Hatch Youth Hostel. Just past the youth hostel fence is a bench for a much earned rest.

4. At the youth hostel take the left hand path, ignoring the path straight ahead with the NT post. Continue to bear left following the yellow sign. The path goes slightly uphill through more attractive woodland with a wide variety of trees. The track widens and you continue until you reach a house on the left hand side and the road ahead.

5. At the house, look to the right to see a barrier across another track and a footpath sign. You can push the buggy under the barrier and now progress along a grassy path. This passes through more woodland and is a lovely earthy track to push the buggy. Go forward at the

Looking back to Polesden Lacy

signpost with the yellow arrow. The path drops down quite steeply so take care. Push the buggy under another barrier to reach a crossroads of paths. Go straight ahead and uphill.

6. When you reach a junction by the 'Road to Dunley' signpost, turn right through a gap in the wooden fence. 100 metres further on go under a wooden barrier. To the left you will pass some fallen tree trunks that are great for older children to play on. Continue ahead gently downhill through the woods.

7. After passing Prospect Lodge, the path bears right downhill through a field. Just by the entrance to the field you will see two benches ahead. From here is a fantastic view towards Polesden Lacey. Bear left up the tarmac lane past Polesden Farm and then right when you reach the crossroads. This last stretch up a sunken lane takes you beneath a thatched bridge that joins the house to its kitchen garden. Shortly after you reach the car park on the right.

Walk 13
Denbies Hillside

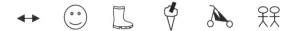

This easy woodland walk along the North Downs Way is punctuated by breathtaking views of the surrounding countryside.

There is a picnic area in Steer Field where the walk starts from, which makes a great spot to relax and enjoy the views. Alternatively you could drop into the neighbouring Denbies Wine Estate for refreshments or even a train ride tour of the vineyard. The vineyard also puts on a range of family activities during school holidays including Punch and Judy shows, pony rides and teddy bears picnics.

Other than needing to lift the buggy over one gate, the paths are wide and flat and navigation couldn't be simpler.

Distance	2.5 miles (a shorter walk is possible)
Allow	1.5 hours
Map	OS 1:250000 Explorer 146. Grid reference TQ142503
Getting there	The walk starts from Denbies Hillside car park on Ranmore Common Road. There is a fee for parking. The closest public transport is Dorking West station, 1.5 miles from the start of the route

1. Go through the kissing gate, which is large enough for a single buggy to get through. Three grassy paths immediately head off in separate directions. Take the middle path to enjoy the best view across the

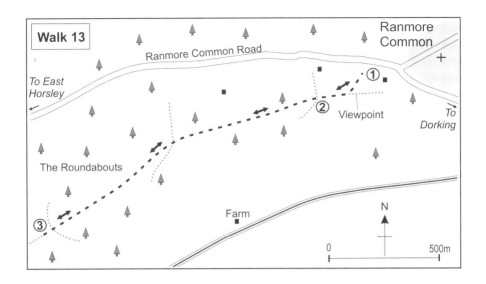

Easy walking along the North Downs Way

valley towards Leith Hill and down to Westcott but make sure you turn right after only 50 metres and head towards the gate into the woodland. You will need to lift the buggy over the gate.

2. Go straight ahead on the wide North Downs Way trail through attractive woodland. After about 400 metres a gap in the tree line reveals again the amazing panorama and the railway line that runs along the foot of the valley – perfect if your children love train-spotting! Having enjoyed the view, you could turn around here and return to the start. Alternatively, go around the fence and continue onwards through the woods.

3. ¾ mile beyond the viewing point, a post in the path marked with the North Downs Way arrow and acorn acts as a turning point. You could go further though the terrain becomes a bit more challenging in places due to exposed tree roots. Return by the same route back to the car park.

Walk 14
Friday Street

A long strenuous walk that takes you through three picturesque sleepy hamlets and past an unexpected waterfall. The countryside is tranquil and beautiful, taking in both sides of the valley cut by the Tillingbourne River including a stretch along the Greensand Way.

It is a fantastic route for walkers happy to take on a challenge; but make sure you are confident about lifting the buggy over tricky stiles, gates and fences as there are multiple crossings. You are likely to be in the outdoors for several hours so ensure you have all the provisions you need. At the end of the walk you can reward yourself with refreshments at the Stephan Langton, a lovely country pub nestled quietly in the Surrey countryside.

Distance	5 miles
Allow	3 hours
Map	OS 1:25000 Explorer 146. Grid reference TQ125457
Getting there	The walk starts from the car park just outside the hamlet of Friday Street which is signposted from the A25 between Wotton and Abinger Hammer. Parking is free

1. Exit the car park and turn right onto the road for 200 metres to reach Mill Pond in the hamlet of Friday Street – there is a footpath from the car park to Friday Street but it is quite tricky terrain so on this occasion it may be preferable to carefully walk on the road. Take the tarmac

footpath just past Pond Cottage and go through the shallow ford (or over the adjacent bridge) before passing the pretty Yew Tree Cottage.

2. You reach a crossroads with a lovely old stone bridge to the left with views of the water meadows downstream. Don't take the path over the bridge but instead continue straight ahead, lifting the buggy over the wooden gate. You are now on a wide track with the stream below to your left. After about ½ mile the track bears right and heads downhill via some easily descended steps.

3. At the bottom of the steps lift the buggy over the stile, cross the stream and walk through the field to reach another stile (it is easier to lift the buggy over the adjacent fence). Wotton House is to your left. Turn right along the tarmac road to reach the main A25 road.

4. Carefully walk right along the road for 50 metres before turning right into Damphurst Lane just past the Wotton Hatch pub. At Wotton Hatch Cottages cross the lane to follow the footpath that runs alongside, with

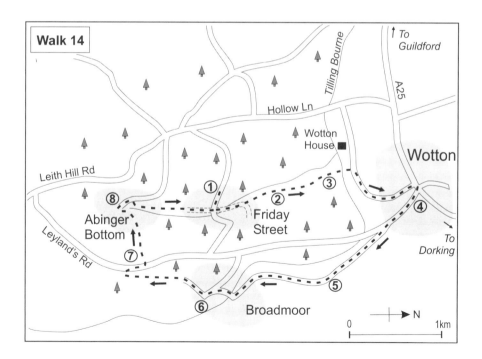

62

Tillingbourne waterfall

farm buildings and cattle fields to your left. When you reach Tillingbourne Lodge join the waymarked Greensand Way straight ahead. Look out for the chicken coop to your left!

5. After about ½ mile you reach a junction. Turn right to continue on the Greensand Way. To your right is a view of the pretty water meadow valley that you crossed earlier by Wotton House. 500 metres beyond the junction you come to the waterfall.

6. When you reach the hamlet of Broadmoor, walk past the cottages and information board. The tarmac road you are on soon ends and becomes a bridleway that gently ascends through woodland. When you reach a junction turn right on a wide track that bears sharply right back on itself, continuing uphill to arrive at a road opposite Wotton Barn.

7. Turn right along the road and soon after go left around a gate to join a footpath that hugs a field boundary. Lift the buggy over two kissing gates and head down the enclosed footpath past a farm and paddock

to the left. When you meet with a quiet road just past Lemon Croft and Beechwood House turn right and follow the road down to Abinger Bottom.

8. Go through the hamlet and just after St John's Cottage take the bridleway off to the right. This woodland track takes you back to Friday Street, passing the Stephan Langton pub which makes a great refreshment stop (you will probably need to leave the buggy outside as the entrance is narrow and there is not much space inside). Continue along the lane to the pond and turn left to return to the car park.

Walk 15
Leith Hill

If you are happy to push your buggy uphill, this woodland walk provides the easiest route to the summit of Leith Hill, the highest point in south-east England (965ft). The paths are generally wide and offer easy walking with a buggy, a few sections are rocky or have exposed tree roots, but nothing too challenging. The grassy area at the hill's summit provides a nice picnic area and fine views towards the south coast in one direction and into central London to the other. The tower itself is owned by the National Trust and can be entered during opening hours (check National Trust website: **www.nationaltrust.org.uk**) for a small admission fee. Standing on the battlements at the top takes you above 1,000 ft and on a fine day offers views for 25 miles. Drinks and snacks are available at the tower when it is open and numerous good country pubs are just a short drive away in Friday Street, Abinger Common and Holmbury St Mary.

Distance	1.5 miles
Allow	1 hour
Map	OS 1:25000 Explorer 146. Grid reference TQ131433
Getting there	The walk starts from Starveall Corner car park on Leith Hill Lane which is easily accessed from the A25 or B2126. Parking is free

1. From the car park head into the woods on the path signposted to the tower. After 200 metres bear right where the path forks.

Leith Hill tower at the walk's summit

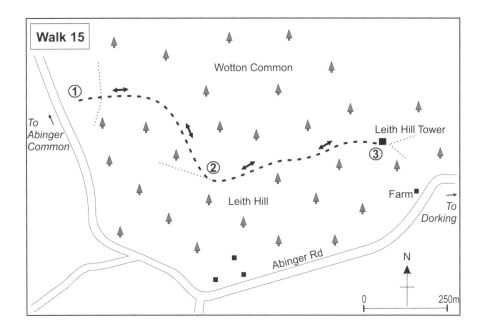

2. When another path intersects after a further 200 metres bear left – you are now on the Greensand Way – and continue upwards until you reach the summit and Leith Hill Tower.

   The tower was built in 1765, extended higher in 1788 and further modified in 1864 to add battlements and a stair turret. From the summit, look out for the monkey puzzle trees growing to the south of the tower and aircraft taking off from Gatwick Airport.

3. Retrace your steps to return to the car park.

Walk 16
Norbury Park

Starting alongside the Mole River, this fun walk in an area of outstanding natural beauty provides a varied landscape including woods, grass and farmland and has the added bonus of a busy railway line cutting through the route for some close to the action train spotting! Towards the end of the walk, a path takes you through the grounds of Bocketts Farm Park. There is an entry fee if you want to see the animals and access all of their play areas and activities but you can visit the lovely café in the barn and some of the outdoor play areas and sandpits for free. If you have brought a picnic, grassland at the halfway point of the route provides a picturesque spot to take a break.

While the majority of this walk is on good tracks, there is a short sharp uphill, and for safety reasons is therefore recommended that the route only be undertaken in dry conditions as it can be slippery. At the time of walking each of the gates you pass through on the walk were unlocked, but should they be padlocked, the adjoining kissing gates are too small to get a buggy through and you will need to lift the buggy over the top.

Distance	2.25 miles
Allow	2 hours
Map	OS 1:50000 Landranger. Grid reference TQ164551
Getting there	The walk starts from Norbury Park car park on Young Street (A246) near Leatherhead. Parking is free

1. From the car park turn left at the information board and go through the gate at the bottom corner of the field. Follow the grassy path that meanders alongside the Mole River before turning left at the top of the field down a wide farm track.

2. At the signpost by the redbrick cottage, turn right through the gate and go under the railway bridge up into the woods. The gentle ascent gets steeper as you near the top of the hill and the path narrows for the final short sharp climb. Take great care as it can be slippery. As you come out of the woodland, turn right onto a quiet road and follow it until you reach the picnic area by Norbury Park Sawmill.

The sawmill is managed by the Surrey Wildlife Trust and manufactures and sells outdoor furniture from English timbers using traditional joinery techniques. All of the information boards and waymarkers you see on this walk have been made here. You can visit the sawmill on weekdays and on occasional open days at weekends.

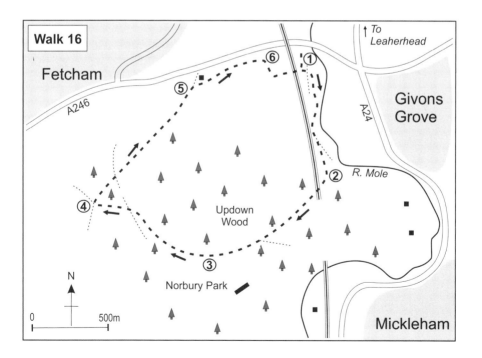

Norbury Park

3. Several paths lead off in different directions, and you should go straight ahead for 150 metres on the path that opens up onto grassland, where there is an information board and bench. This would be a good point to stop for a break. Head down the hill on the main track, continuing straight ahead when you reach the bottom.

4. At the junction close to Roaringhouse Farm, turn right down the bridleway.

   Keep a look out in the fields to the right for llamas and ponies from Bocketts Farm.

5. When you reach Bocketts Farm turn right through the grounds. If you are not stopping for refreshments or going into the farm, go past the café area and take the footpath that heads up between the trees.

6. Go through the wooden gate and turn right into the field. The path is narrow and difficult to negotiate with the buggy. It may be easier to

carry the buggy for this short stretch. Turn left after 50 metres through the field towards the railway line and through the tunnel to return to the car park.

Walk 17
Headley Heath

This National Trust owned heathland provides great routes for buggies with wide and mostly flat paths (so long as a descent into the valley is avoided). This short circular walk crosses the heath and follows paths through shaded woodland, including a great view of Box Hill. You might also be lucky enough to spot one of the grazing highland cattle, though I wouldn't get too close! The open space by the car park is popular for picnics but you will find quieter spots on the route. There is a snack bar in the car park selling snacks and drinks but has no indoor seating.

Distance	1.75 miles
Allow	1 hour
Map	OS 1:25000 Explorer 146. Grid reference TQ205538
Getting there	The walk starts from the main National Trust car park on Headley Common Road (B2033). There is a fee for parking (free for NT members)

1. With your back to the road, take the path straight across the small area of heath by the car park towards a gate. Continue through the gate (marked with a yellow National Trust arrow) and gently descend the chalk path bordered by ferns, oak and silver birch trees.

2. After 300 metres the now grassy path forks but you should continue straight ahead towards the prominent silver birch tree. You will encounter various crossings but ignore them until the path meets a

Finding dandelions to blow is always fun!

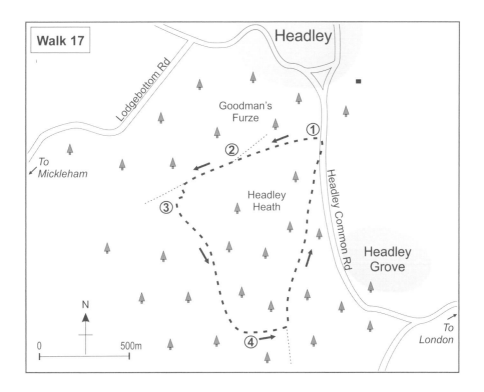

major gravel track. Turn right onto the track. This soon reaches a clearing known as the Pyramids where five paths converge and views across the valley towards Box Hill can be enjoyed.

3. Take the second path on your left which is marked by the post with a painted blue arrow. The initial descent is short lived and the mostly shaded path continues with flat and gentle uphill sections for half a mile until a major intersection is reached.

4. Cross over the first intersection and then at the second, almost immediately after, turn left. After 100 metres turn left again and continue on this wide path through peaceful woodland back to the car park. You will pass a small pond along the way but sadly it does not seem to be home to any ducks.

Walk 18
Reigate Hill

This short walk follows the North Downs Way across the top of Reigate and Colley Hills taking in fine views as far away as the South Downs. It is an out and back route, though there is an option for a slight detour on the return trip to enjoy the alternative and even more dramatic views of the steep escarpment. Using the North Downs Way means it is easy to navigate and the terrain good for buggies – you could get away with not using an all-terrain model. It is also a nice route for toddling tots and you may see some grazing cattle, which are huge!

For refreshments, there is a snack bar in Wray Lane car park with picnic benches and deck chairs outside but no indoor seating. They serve a good selection of hot and cold drinks, sandwiches and home-made cakes. Toilets are located next to the kiosk but there are no baby changing facilities.

Distance	2 miles
Allow	1.5 hours
Map	OS 1:25000 Explorer 146. Grid reference TQ258518
Getting there	The walk starts from Wray Lane car park at the top of Reigate Hill. Parking is free. If travelling by public transport, you can take the 420 or 460 bus up Reigate Hill. You'll then need to cross the A217 via the footbridge

1. Cross over the A217 via the footbridge behind the kiosk and head through the woodland on a wide track. Shortly after passing the row of cottages on Fort Lane you will come to Reigate Fort.

   The fort is one of sixteen look out points along the North Downs built in the 1890s to protect London from potential foreign invasion. It was used in the First World War for ammunition storage and stationed Canadian troops in the Second World War. You can wander round the fort where there are National Trust information boards that tell the history.

2. After a further 700 metres along this pretty woodland trail go through the gate which takes you to Colley Hill. The first thing you'll see on the open downland is the Inglis Memorial. The view from the memorial is quite spectacular and the surrounding grassy downs are a great spot for a picnic. When you're ready to move on, continue along the main path taking in the views until you reach a gate by a sign for Colley Hill.

   The memorial was donated to the Borough of Reigate in 1909 by Lieutenant Colonel Sir Robert William Inglis. It was originally a

Grassland at the top of Colley Hill

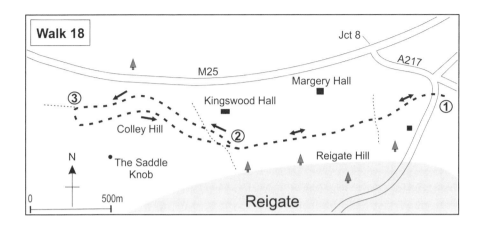

drinking fountain for horses, standing at the top of the original main route over Reigate Hill. Now restored, its ornately decorated ceiling represents the heavens and its viewpoint indicator shows the major southerly landmarks.

3. From the gate you can either return back to the car park via the same route or turn left before the gate along the grassy path and then almost immediately left again. This route back to the memorial provides a dramatic view of the escarpment. Head towards the bench beneath the tree from where the memorial should be in sight. Take any one of the grassy paths and when you reach the gate, head through it and retrace the track back through the woods passing the fort to the car park.

Walk 19
Gatton Park

    WC

Ownership of Gatton Park is split between the Gatton Trust and the National Trust and this route takes you round the woods, parkland and ponds of the National Trust owned area. In spite of some undulations, the terrain is relatively easy on mostly wide tracks. With the same start point as the Reigate Hill route, the two walks can be combined or undertaken separately. Gatton Park has an entirely different feel to the route across the tops of Reigate and Colley Hills so can make for an interesting blend of landscapes – it's also far less popular with walkers, making it a very peaceful alternative.

Gatton Park has an interesting history having been landscaped by Lancelot 'Capability' Brown in the mid 18th century and last owned by Sir Jeremiah Colman (he of mustard fame). One of the most interesting and unexpected sights on the walk is the Millennium Stones; a modern stone circle created by Richard Kindersley to mark the double millennium.

Visits to the Gatton Trust Estate are possible on the first Sunday of each month between February and October, with guided tours through the landscaped gardens. The cost is £3.50 for adults.

Distance	2 miles
Allow	1.5 hours
Map	OS 1:25000 Landranger. Grid reference TQ258518
Getting there	The walk starts from Wray Lane car park at the top of Reigate Hill. Parking is free. If travelling by public transport, you can take the 420 or 460 bus up Reigate Hill. You'll then need to cross the A217 via the footbridge

For refreshments, there is a snack bar in Wray Lane car park with picnic benches and deck chairs outside but no indoor seating. They serve a good selection of hot and cold drinks, sandwiches and home-made cakes. Toilets are located next to the kiosk but there are no baby changing facilities.

1. Head back to the car park entrance and cross the road to the National Trust sign for Gatton Park. Follow the path downhill gently, ignoring the option of turning left. When the path forks again after 50 metres go left where the trees soon open to reveal a view down Wingate Hill.

2. At this viewpoint, turn sharply right and continue downhill past a stile to your left from where more of the parkland comes into sight, including St Andrew's Church, Gatton Hall and the Royal Alexander and Albert School. Remain on the track that hugs the perimeter of the field as it descends and then rises on the other side to re-enter the woods, going through a gate part way up the ascent.

3. At the summit, the fern lined track bears left and soon begins to descend again before forking. You can take either path as both reach the same end point but the left hand fork provides a further view of

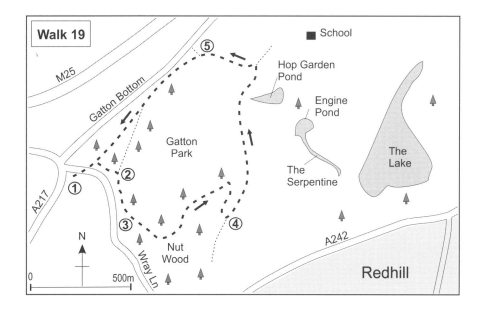

Easy route finding along the North Downs Way

the park and is an easier descent. The track heads into dense woodland that feels somewhat dark and spooky even on a bright summer's day. It then sweeps round to the right where you will find a bench at the viewpoint.

4. At the bottom of the hill, go round a gate, and bear left along a wide flat track through the landscape you just viewed from the woods. After 500 metres go round a metal gate and past the pretty Hop Garden Pond. Follow the track as it bears right in the direction of the school and then sharply left at the Millennium Stones. Go round a second metal gate and back up into the woods.

Gatton Park was the chosen site for the Millennium Stones as it lies on the Pilgrims Way. Each of the ten stones represents a 200 year time period and is inscribed with quotes from that era, beginning with works from St John's Gospel and ending with T S Elliot.

5. Turn left before the road at the National Trust sign for Gatton Park. When you reach a fork after 300 metres go right onto the Millennium Trail to return to the car park through Great Buck Wood.

Walk 20
Godstone

A short easy stroll that takes you past a number of pretty ponds and some beautiful cottages close to Godstone village. The walk starts from Godstone Green pond which is a great spot for duck feeding. But if you're looking for more animals than just ducks, Godstone Farm is half a mile outside of the village and is home to all the usual animals as well as indoor and outdoor play areas for all ages, sandpits and tractor rides. This walk offers the chance to wind down after the excitement of a visit to the farm! The village itself has a shop, café and pubs and the green would make a good spot for a picnic.

Distance	2 miles
Allow	1 hour
Map	OS 1:25000 Explorer 146. Grid reference TQ350515
Getting there	Parking is available in the village next to Godstone Green Pond on the A25. Parking is free

1. From the car park cross over the road and take the path that starts to the right of the White Hart pub. The tarmac path takes you past Bay Pond on your left and comes out opposite the grade I listed St Nicholas Church. It's well worth pausing here for a few moments to admire the church, St Mary's Chapel and almshouses and their pretty gardens.

2. Head through the churchyard on the path to the right of the church, passing between the gap in the fence at the bottom of the graveyard to follow the path around the pond (Glebe Water).

3. Just before the conifer trees turn left to head through the meadow. Cross the meadow and go through the gap in the hedge before heading down the hill, first following the line of the fence and then the hedge before turning left onto Leigh Place Lane.

4. Just before the road bridge crossing the path, turn right down a bridleway which bears round to the right and passes close to the tranquil Leigh Place Pond. Go through the white gate and past White Mill House before turning right onto the bridleway signposted for the Greensand Way. You then have to cross the ford as the bridge over it is too narrow to go over with a buggy.

5. At the end of the bridleway turn right onto the road (where there is a pavement) passing the pretty Hythe Cottages on the opposite side of

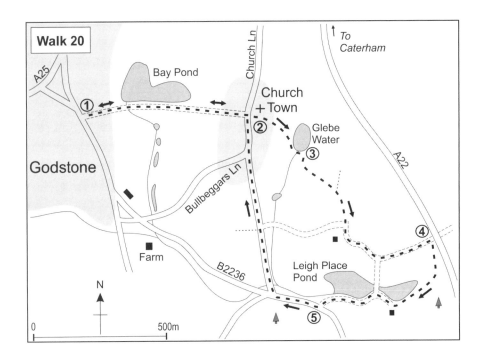

The entrance to St Nicolas church

the road. After 100 metres turn right down Church Lane which is dotted with beautiful old cottages to return to St Nicholas Church. This area is known as the Enterdent and the properties remain relatively unchanged since their construction in the mid 19th century. At the church turn left back along the footpath you arrived on earlier to return to Godstone village.

Walk 21
Limpsfield Chart

Beginning in evergreen woodland of The High Chart, this undulating route on the Surrey-Kent border takes you through tranquil bluebell woods, past ancient beech trees and alongside fields of cattle. The village of Limpsfield Chart makes for a good half way point, complete with a welcoming pub (The Carpenters Arms) and children's playground next to the cricket field. The field adjacent to the car park at the start/finish would also make a pleasant spot for a picnic.

A large network of footpaths criss-cross the High Chart woods bringing the potential to get rather lost. To avoid going off course, the route follows three well signposted long-distance paths: initially the Tandridge Border Path, which links with the Greensand Way and finally the Vanguard Way. Make sure you look out for the markers and retrace your steps to relocate the route if necessary.

Distance	2.5 miles
Allow	2 hours
Map	OS 1:25000 Explorer 147. Grid reference TQ430529
Getting there	The walk starts from the first car park you reach on Moorhouse Road having turned off the A25 between Limpsfield and Westerham. Parking is free. You could park further along Moorhouse Road closer to Limpsfield Chart and join the walk at point 3 but parking spaces are more limited

The terrain is a mix of wide flat paths and a few hills with more challenging ground underfoot, including plenty of exposed tree routes. However, the most difficult element of this walk is likely to be muddy tracks after rain.

1. From the car park cross the road and go through the open gate by the sign for High Chart. Immediately turn right down the narrow footpath signposted 'Tandridge Border Path'. The route soon begins to descend through dense pine trees and the path becomes difficult to identify amongst the carpet of pine needles. This is a magical spot when the sun filters through the trees giving everything a rusty glow. Head downhill until you reach the sunken bridleway.

   Look left along the bridleway to find the yellow arrow that points you up the opposite side of the valley. It is a bumpy path through the pines. At the top, three paths join together – go straight ahead, ignoring the right hand fork after 20 metres. Cross over the major path and continue along the 'Tandridge Border Path'. When you reach a major intersection, turn left onto a wide path (still signposted TBP). After a further 400 metres you reach major intersections where you cease following the Tandridge Border Path.

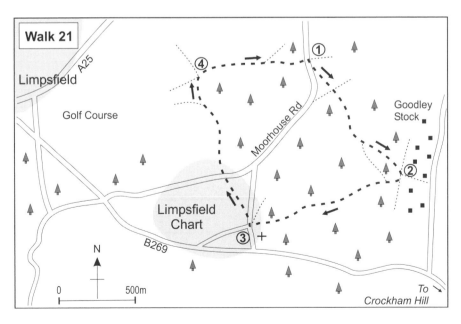

2. Turn right to begin a ¾ mile stretch along the Greensand Way that takes you to the village of Limpsfield Chart – look out for the yellow arrows marked with a 'GW' in the centre. After 150 metres bear left along a track that gently descends and crosses over two major intersections. When you reach a fork in the track (where disconcertingly there isn't a Greensand Way signpost to point you in the right direction), bear left around the large crater and then turn right when it meets with a wider path to arrive at the village.

3. Turn right onto Moorhouse Road and then bear left onto Stoneleigh Road, passing the row of houses. Follow the footpath past the playground and cross the road to join a bridleway on the opposite side. You are now walking on the Vanguard Way. Head downhill and when the path forks after passing the ancient beech hedge stay on the path closest to the fields to your left. At a second fork further down the hill continue straight ahead on the Vanguard Way.

4. At the bottom of the hill turn right (departing from the Vanguard Way). In spring and early summer the fields to your left will be full of

Enjoying the wide open fields at Limpsfield

flowering rapeseed. Go through the gate and cross the field to another gate. The path continues left with the cattle field adjacent. When the now sandy track starts to ascend, fork right and continue up through the ferns and past another beech hedge to return to the car park.

Walk 22
Woldingham and Marden Park Woods

With easy access by public transport or car, this easy to follow route takes you through pretty woods and farmland with views of lush rolling hills and the North Downs. A potentially slow walk given the full complement of farm animals in the fields within the first half mile to practice your moos and oinks with! There are also many opportunities to spot wildlife en route – during our last time here we saw roe deer and foxes. We also spent quite a long time picking the luscious blackberries which grow along many of the paths, so don't forget a container if you're here in August or September!

Steps and stiles need to be negotiated making it a two person walk but apart from a small handful of steep sections it is a relatively easy walk with long stretches of good paths through woodland.

There are no facilities en route but Knights Garden Centre is just a few minutes walk or drive from the start of the route on Woldingham Road and has a well-stocked café and toilets.

Distance	4 miles
Allow	2-3 hours
Map	OS 1:25000 Explorer 146. Grid reference TQ359563
Getting there	Take the train to Woldingham Station or park on Church Farm Road adjacent to the station. Parking is free

1. From the station turn right up Church Road. Just before Church Road Farm turn right over the railway bridge and follow the road round to the left towards Marden Park Farm. Although early in the walk, you might linger here for a while as the fields are home to cows, sheep, goats, pigs and chickens! Once you are ready to continue, the road quickly turns into a bridleway and heads gently uphill with lovely views of the valley.

Views of the valley near the start of the route

2. When you reach a junction by a gate, carry on straight ahead down through the woods. The path exits the woods at Woldingham School, go past the small cemetary on your left, cross the quiet road and over the stile opposite into the field.

   The catholic girls Woldingham School has been located at this site since the 1940s and has several notable alumnae – actresses Carey Mulligan and Rachel Weisz and celebrity chef Clarissa Dickson-Wright (expelled!) to name a few.

3. Keeping the trees to your left, head up through the field, turning left when you reach the top towards the kissing gate. Rather than going

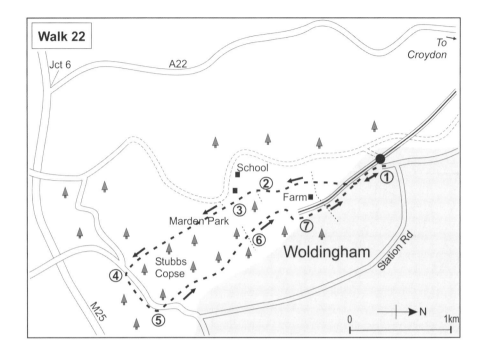

through the gate you should be able to push your buggy under the adjacent wooden barrier (though you may need to tilt the buggy back a little to get the handle bar through!) Turn immediately right and follow the main path through the woods (ignoring any turn offs to the right or left) for about half a mile until you meet with a road.

4. Turn left and follow the road for 100 metres where you find a footpath off to the right of the road signed North Downs Way. This path runs parallel to the road before turning right down a short, sharp and rather bumpy hill and then left at the bottom. You will soon come to an opening in the wood where there is a fine view across towards Tandridge, sadly marred by an equally good view of the M25! Continue swiftly onwards back into the woods, turning left when you come to steps that will take you back up to the road.

5. Cross the road and the car park opposite and go through the gate signed Marden Park Woodland Trust. Ignoring the path that heads through another gate to the left, head down the hill on a good, wide

track. Continue straight ahead when you come to paths heading off to the right to Great Church Wood and St Agatha's Church. You will likely see grazing goats on the slopes below the path and there are a few benches where you can take a break to enjoy the lovely views across the valley.

You could take the short detour to St Agatha's Church but it does involve a flight of steps to reach it. The small church built in 1832 is the highest in Surrey, while the ash tree growing beside it is thought to be 900 years old.

6. Turn left on the path heading back into woodland (signposted to Woldingham Station) and then right soon after (again in the direction of the station). Take care on the descent which is initially narrow and steep but soon becomes a much more gradual downhill.

7. Cross the stile at the bottom of the path and turn left back across the railway. Follow the path over one final stile and turn left back onto Church Road for an easy ¾ mile stroll back to the station.

Walk 23
Happy Valley

A beautiful but challenging walk down (and back up!) Happy Valley. The variety of terrain makes for an interesting route including woodland paths, farmland and grassy slopes as well as the option to visit the medieval Chaldon Church. It's best saved for good weather as many of the tracks turn into a quagmire after rain making it virtually impossible to make progress with a buggy. In fine weather most of the paths are highly accessible, only a few short stretches are narrow or have exposed tree roots.

The full walk is four miles and although a shorter route is possible it is equally strenuous, avoiding only a few of the uphill stretches. Whichever route you choose, the Fox Pub close to the start offers good food and a nice garden.

Distance	4 miles
Allow	2.5 hours
Map	OS 1:25000 Explorer 146. Grid reference TQ318568
Getting there	The walk starts from the car park at the end of Fox Lane off Coulsdon Road (B2030). Parking is free. By public transport, you can take the 404 or 466 to The Fox Pub which only adds a couple of hundred metres to the route

1. From the car park take the tarmac path alongside the trim trail. After 350 metres the tarmac ends and you should take the wide track downhill through the trees. It soon bears right and opens up to give beautiful views of Happy Valley.

2. Continue straight ahead on the grassy path across the side of the valley which is signposted to Farthing Down. 200 metres ahead you pass through a small wooded area; upon reaching a picnic bench and signpost you should head diagonally downhill to the valley floor and then turn right along the wide grassy trail.

Looking across Happy Valley

3. After about 600 metres along this low level trail bear left where there is a further signpost for Farthing Down. There is an extremely steep track heading directly up the opposite side of the valley that you have come from – don't take this route but instead follow the narrower path that heads diagonally right up the hillside. It's still challenging, with some exposed tree routes, but by far the easier option. At the top is a well positioned bench for a recovery break and views back across the valley.

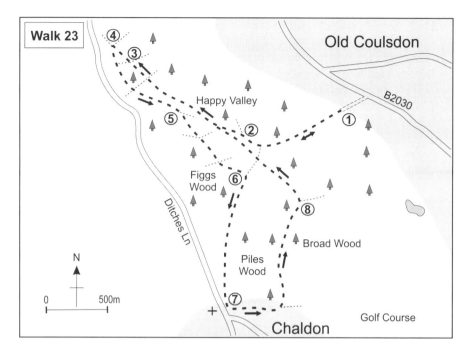

4. When you are ready to resume the walk, turn sharp left along an initially tricky path which soon becomes a much easier wide track through the lovely Devilsden Wood. When you reach a fork 300 metres after entering the woods, take the left path heading gently downhill towards Happy Valley.

5. When you exit the woods continue across the top of the valley on the grassy slope with the trees to your right.

   If you prefer a shorter walk you could at this point head diagonally down the slope to the bottom of the valley and retrace your steps back up the other side.

   When you meet with the treeline ahead, don't turn down towards the valley but cut through the trees via a rugged path up to your right and then return to the grassland.

6. At the end of this next stretch of grass take a sharp right uphill and pass through the corn fields. When you reach the opposite side of the

field, rather than going straight ahead through the woods, turn left and continue on a farm track until it meets with the road. If you would like to visit the pretty Chaldon Church, turn right onto the road and then left at the signpost for Chaldon.

7. If you are not taking the detour to the church, continue around the perimeter of the field and then left through Piles Wood. The path heads steadily downhill to the bottom of the valley.

8. Take a sharp left to follow the grassy track along the valley floor for ¾ mile until you reach the foot of the path that you came down from the start of the walk – you could take one of the alternative paths up the valley that you see as you walk along the valley floor but they are far steeper. Whichever path you take, once at the top of the valley, retrace your steps back to the car park.

Walk 24
Banstead Woods

Banstead Woods is an ancient woodland with numerous footpaths. On this walk you will pass a wide variety of tree species, while in springtime the woodland floor becomes a carpet of bluebells.

Most of the route is on wide tracks and the few undulations are not too taxing. If you enjoy this walk but are keen for a greater challenge, every Saturday morning a 5k trail run takes place in the woods that you can participate in with a buggy!

For refreshments, the child friendly Ramblers Rest pub is on Outwood Lane which you can either walk or drive to from Holly Lane car park.

Distance	2.5 miles
Allow	1.5 hours
Map	OS 1:25000 Explorer 146. Grid reference TQ273582
Getting there	Parking is available at Holly Lane car park (free) on the B2219. The closest train station is Chipstead, 250 metres from the start of the walk

1. From the top left hand corner of the car park go through the gate and up through the meadows towards the woods. Take the signposted track to Perrots Farm and almost immediately after turn right at the signpost for the Banstead Wood nature trail. Once through the gate, turn left to head up a fairly strenuous hill for 200 metres and then turn right.

Path through the ferns at Banstead Woods

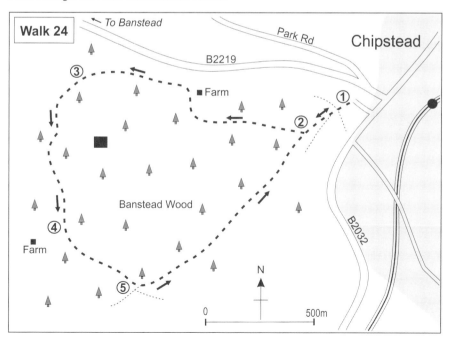

2. Follow this path for ¼ mile, ignoring all junctions on either side. The path eventually curves to the right and heads downhill, meeting with a four way junction. Continue straight ahead and go up the short hill. Take the path that bears right back downhill and then curves left to a grassy area with a small orchard to the left.

3. 300 metres beyond the orchard you reach a road. Cross it and continue along the path that initially runs through rhododendrons and then dense woodland. The path narrows and becomes bordered by ferns as it bears back to the left.

4. When you arrive at a wider path turn right and after 200 metres emerge at a fine beech tree by a clearing. Turn left here and then right by a bench, remaining on the wide track. Go past the pond, ignoring the turn off here to the left.

5. 50 metres beyond the pond turn left and follow this track along the perimeter of the woods for ½ mile to return to the car park.

Walk 25
Banstead Countryside Walk

A second walk in Banstead, starting at the same point as the woodland walk, but taking in more varied landscape including farmland and chalk hills. Some lovely views are to be had across the valley to Chipstead. We most recently enjoyed this walk in spring when the bluebells were in bloom and the new foliage glowed in the glorious late afternoon sun. A great time to be out walking.

The terrain is varied with a mix of good wide tracks, narrower paths and exposed tree routes. With several stiles en route and a couple of very short but very steep inclines, where it's actually easier to carry the buggy, this is a two person walk and single buggies only.

For refreshments, the child friendly Ramblers Rest pub is on Outwood Lane which you can either walk or drive to. You could even start and end the walk here but it's a steep climb up the valley to reach the route at point 3.

Distance	3.5 miles
Allow	2 hours
Map	OS 1:25000 Explorer 146. Grid reference SU892533
Getting there	Parking is available at Holly Lane car park (free) on the B2219. The closest train station is Chipstead, 250 metres from the start of the walk

1. From the top left hand corner of the car park go through the gate and up through the meadows towards the woods. Take the signposted track to Perrots Farm and enjoy some great views across the valley as you head gradually uphill for about 300 metres.

2. When you reach a junction in the path continue straight ahead on the 'summer route' path. Ignore any turn offs to the right that go up onto the meadow and continue along the pretty tree lined trail, being careful with the exposed tree roots. At the crossroads follow the path to Farms Rough – you'll probably see sheep grazing in the field to your left. Along this path is the route up from the Ramblers Rest should you choose to start the walk from the pub. Bear left downhill after 200 metres and then immediately right after a descent of only 20 metres or so – signposted to Banstead Woods. The path is narrow and bumpy for 100 metres and then steadily heads uphill as it opens up to a pretty clearing before re-entering the woods.

3. The route then follows a trail marked 'main route' where the path is narrow and bordered with rhododendrons and bluebells in spring. You

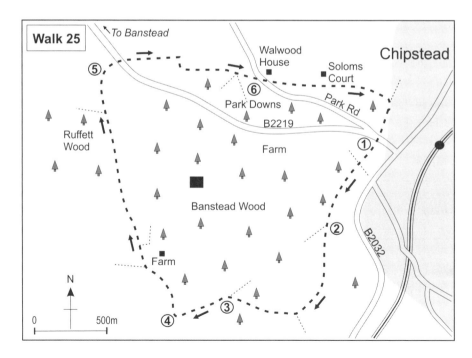

Looking across farmland from the adjacent track

will need to go round several trees that have fallen across the path and it may be easier to occasionally carry the buggy here. Ignore the turn off left and continue until the path turns right and you cross a small stile.

4. You can now see Perrots Farm straight ahead as the path hugs the woods to your right. Cross the stile to the right of the farm and then another on the opposite side of the farm road. Continue 600 metres on the path through farmland and then along the edge of Ruffet Wood for a further 350 metres until you go around a stile and descend the grassy slope towards Holly Lane. Before reaching the road, you need to negotiate a tricky stile and a couple of very short steep sections.

5. At the road, cross with care and go straight up the footpath opposite. This goes round the top of the field, descending slightly on the far side of the field before cutting through a marked footpath on the left taking you onto Park Downs. Follow the top path through the trees ignoring any turn offs until 100 metres after the Banstead Commons notice

board where you turn left and reach another road crossing at Park Road.

6. Rejoin the path immediately opposite (it's quite a steep climb to get back up to the path) and continue for 750 metres until you reach a wall straight ahead – turn right and head downhill back to the car park.

Walk 26
Epsom Downs

    WC

This pleasant, easy walk starts from Epsom racecourse, home of the Derby, and meanders through downland and woods on good bridleways with only easy undulations to challenge you. Located just outside the endless London suburbs, it feels like the perfect get away from city life, though great views of the city can be seen from Grand Stand Road, a short detour from the start of the route.

Children will enjoy watching horses training on the racecourse and out for hacks on the surrounding bridleways. You might also spot model aircraft being flown. Older children could also cycle this route as it is entirely on bridleways, some specifically part of the national cycle network.

The Downs Lunch Box kiosk at the start of the route serves snacks and drinks but has no indoor seating.

Distance	3 miles
Allow	1.5 hours
Map	OS 1:25000 Explorer 146. Grid reference TQ224584
Getting there	The walk starts by the mini roundabout on Tattenham Corner Road (B290). Parking is available at the start of the walk. Use the free car park on the south side of the road to avoid having to cross the busy B290. If this is not possible, park behind the 'Downs Lunch Box' kiosk and cross at the pelican crossing 75 metres to your left. If arriving by train, Tattenham Corner and Epsom Downs stations are a short walk away

1. The walk begins by crossing the race track between furlong markers 3 and 4 and follows the bridleway straight ahead marked by the National Cycle Route 22. After about 300 metres cross the race track for a second time, this time by furlong marker 8. Continue on the path straight ahead, with trees to your right (ignoring a path that heads left after 150 metres).

2. Soon after entering woodland the path bears sharply right but you should follow the bridleway signposted left. You quickly emerge from the woods to fine views of rolling farmland (and the distant hum of the M25!). Keep following the bridleway which re-enters the woods for a short time and then descends to meet with a 'Racehorses only' sign at a six-way intersection.

3. At the intersection take the signposted bridleway immediately to the left of the path that is marked with the Cycle Route 22 sign and gently

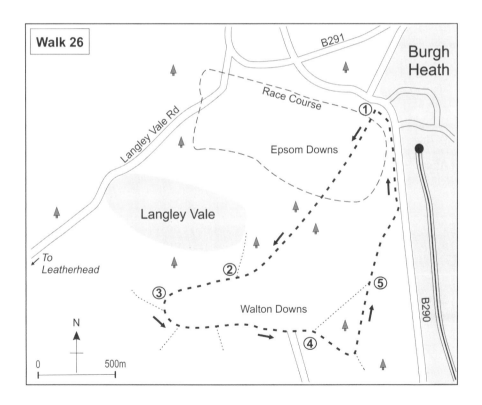

descend through pretty woodland. At the bottom of the path bear left, passing by waymarkers indicating right towards Walton Road. You soon come to another junction in the path where you should follow the signpost to Ebbisome Lane. The bridleway now runs parallel with an exercise track for racehorses which runs alongside on your left.

4. After 400 metres when the bridleway bears round to the left, continue straight ahead through the trees, across the grassy area and back into woodland. When you reach a signposted junction take the bridleway to the left which heads gently uphill on a slightly rocky path following signs to Epsom Lane North.

5. When the path emerges from the trees and meets again with the main bridleway turn right and head towards the houses in view. This track returns you to the start of the walk though the last 100 metres are on a grass verge by the side of a busy road so take care.

Walk 27
Ashtead and Epsom Commons

This is an easy route which begins on Epsom Common but crosses into neighbouring Ashtead Common, making use of wide flat tracks and sections of grassy bridleways which can be bumpy and boggy. As the commons lie on a thick layer of London clay, it might be best to save this walk for good weather as pushing a buggy along waterlogged tracks can be a real struggle after rain.

Ashtead Common is one of several open spaces in the London area managed by the City of London Corporation, while Epsom Common is managed by the local council. The bridleways and footpaths of both are extremely well maintained and signposted and take you through a variety of landscapes: woods, heath and grassland as well as ponds and streams.

Distance	2.5 miles
Allow	1.5 hours
Map	OS 1:25000 Explorer 161 and 146. Grid reference TQ184612
Getting there	Parking is available at Stew Ponds car park (free) off the Christ Church Road (B280). Alternatively, you could arrive by train at Ashtead station and join the walk at point 5. The station is located adjacent to Ashtead Common and a 10 minute walk up numbered bridleway 33 will reach the main route

Together Epsom and Ashtead Commons form a Site of Special Scientific Interest and nature reserve due to their importance for nature conservation. It is most notably home to communities of breeding birds, including woodpeckers, owls and nuthatches; and 300-400 year old pollarded oak trees (pollarding involves regularly cutting trees at head height to produce a crop of fodder, fuel and timber). You will likely hear a woodpecker or two and probably also see the local population of parakeets.

While you're in the area you could also visit Horton Park Children's Farm which has a range of animals and play areas.

1. Go around the gate closest to the car park entrance where there is an information board and map of the commons. Head along the wide gravel track. You soon arrive at Stew Pond, a popular spot for ducks and fishermen. Turn right at the pond and head up the gentle winding slope that enters woodland.

   Look across to the other side of the pond and you will see some wooden steps which lead up to Great Pond, a tranquil haven for wildlife that is well worth making the short detour either at the start or end of the route.

2. After 200 metres turn left onto the path signposted 'Epsom Common all weather path'.

   At this intersection you'll see one of several coal tax posts located on the common. In total, 280 of these posts were erected around the outskirts of London in the 1860s to mark the boundary within which the City of London levied a tax on coal imports.

   The path now flattens and meanders through dense woodland of silver birch, holly and oak trees. When you reach a fork after about half a mile, take the right hand path, passing by the small Ashtead Common Pond.

3. After gradually descending for a further ¼ mile you reach a crossroads where you should take the right hand path signposted 'Concessionary Ride Ashtead Common'. There is a map on an information board on the opposite path for you to locate where you are within the commons. The wide track continues through woodland which opens out after 200

metres to reveal a wooden bridge crossing the Rye Brooke tributary of the Mole River.

The noticeboard by the bridge provides information on the river restoration work that is taking place to sustain this wetland habitat.

Don't follow the path across the bridge but remain on the main path, ignoring all further intersections. Shortly after the track bears right, it splits four ways – continue ahead where the terrain turns to grass bordered by bracken.

4. Soon after passing two lovely oak trees to the right you reach a sign for Bridleway 33. Turn left down the hill here if you are returning to Ashtead Station or right if you are parked at Stew Pond. Follow this lovely peaceful wide winding track, which can be wet and bumpy in places.

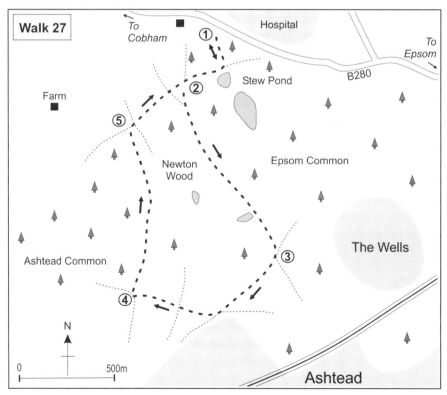

Lovely oak trees along the Ashtead Common 'concessionary ride'

5. At the end of the track you reach Chessington View with a pleasant panorama of rolling farmland and the woodland beyond. Turn right here, keeping the farmland to your left where you will likely spot grazing cows and horses. After ½ mile you will be back at Stew Pond.

Walk 28
Ham Riverside

The Thames towpath is a great place to walk with little ones as there is so much to see. The river itself is a hive of human activity, particularly in summer, with serious rowers and canoeists sharing the water with day trippers in hire boats armed with picnic hampers and bottles of wine... you might even see a Venetian gondola as well as the occasional brave swimmer! And of course there are a wealth of ducks, swans and herons. This section of the towpath also takes you past several notable buildings, including Ham, Orleans and Marble Hill Houses, some of which you can visit. Though busy on weekends, you'll find the riverside a tranquil location if you are out for a weekday stroll.

This is an easy out-and-back walk which can be extended to a circular route by taking the Hammerton foot ferry to the Middlesex side of the

Distance	1.75 miles (2.5 miles extended route)
Allow	1.5 hours
Map	OS 1:25000 Explorer 161. Grid reference TQ169731
Getting there	The walk starts from the free public car park at the end of Ham Street. Turn off the A307 which runs between Richmond and Kingston at Ham Common. If travelling by public transport, you could undertake the route in reverse by arriving into Richmond station and making the short walk from the town centre to the tow path. In total, this will add about a mile and a half to the walk.

river and returning across Richmond Bridge. There will need to be two of you to carry the buggy down the steps onto the ferry. Interesting extensions can be made either northwards to Kew or south to Teddington Lock. While there are no refreshments en route for the short walk, nearby Richmond has a wealth of eateries, many of which are located on the towpath (which you will pass on the extended route).

1. From the car park turn right along the tow path which can be muddy after rain. Immediately opposite is Orleans House and after 100 metres appears Ham House.

   Ham House is a National Trust property. Built in the 17th century, it was home to the Duchess of Lauderdale who is said to still haunt the building. The house was at the heart of civil war politics and has lovely gardens restored to their original splendour.

2. If you are taking the longer route, the steps to the Hammerton foot ferry are by Ham House.

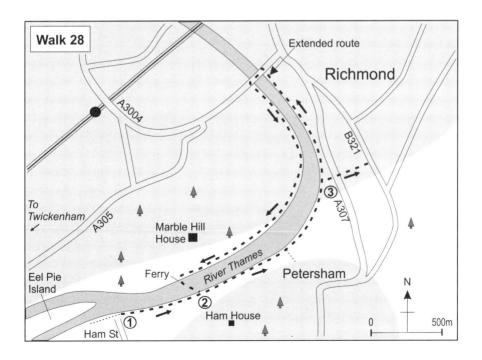

The ferry operates year round at weekends from 10am to 6.30pm (or dusk if earlier) and on weekdays between February and October from 10am to 6pm. Just stand at the top of the steps and the ferryman will cross the river to collect you. Cost is 60p per adult, 30p per child but buggies travel free!

The short route continues along the Surrey side of the river with views of Marble Hill House set within Marble Hill park.

Marble Hill is the last complete survivor of the elegant villas and gardens which bordered the Thames between Richmond and Hampton Court in the 18th century. It was originally inhabited by Henrietta Howard, mistress of King George II when he was Prince of Wales. The house is open to visitors at weekends between April and November.

As the river bears left you reach a launching point for boats - a good spot for duck feeding. It is also at this point in the walk that

Watching the ever changing river scene

you meet with Petersham Meadow, home of grazing cattle. From here is a view up Richmond Hill to its many splendid buildings including The Royal Star and Garter, home for disabled ex-servicemen and women; the Petersham Hotel and the Hill's terrace.

3. Continue along the towpath with the meadow to your right until you reach Buccleuch Gardens. From here you can either turn round and retrace your steps back to Ham or, if you are feeling energetic take the short detour across the road and straight up the steep path to Richmond Hill terrace.

The panorama from the top is worth the effort and is the only view in England to be protected by an Act of Parliament. Described by Sir Walter Scott as an "unrivalled landscape" you will be able to look back at the route you have taken along the Thames and far beyond.

You will need to head back down the hill to the towpath and retrace your steps back to the car park.

Extended route
Once across the river, turn right and continue along the towpath until you reach Richmond Bridge. Cross the bridge and return to the towpath on the Surrey side of the river and follow it all the way back to Ham (1¼ miles).

Walk 29
Richmond Park

Richmond Park is the largest of London's royal parks and its 2,500 acres provide a varied landscape of hills, woods and grassland. Wildlife is in abundance with opportunities to spot resident deer and birdlife including parakeets and ducks – so bring bread for feeding! Although in London, at times it is easy to imagine you're on an African savannah!

There are paths aplenty within the park and this walk aims to take in some of its highlights, enjoy quieter areas and avoid as much as possible the road that circles the park. The route follows both good paths and some more challenging terrain, including two uphill sections. There are several road crossings on this route but the speed limit is restricted and drivers tend to be very cautious and considerate of walkers, cyclists and deer alike. The sheer number of paths within the park can make

Distance	4.5 miles
Allow	3 hours
Map	OS 1:25000 Explorer 161. Grid reference TQ187728
Getting there	The walk starts from Pembroke Lodge within Richmond Park where there is car parking (busy at weekends). Parking is free. If using public transport, Richmond station is the closest though you will then need to either take a bus up Richmond Hill or walk to enter the park via Richmond Gate. Walking from the station would add 1.5 miles onto the walk in each direction

navigating a little tricky at times but even if you do lose the route you are unlikely to go too far off track.

The walk also takes you past the beautiful Isabella Plantation and it is well worth taking the time to stroll inside this ornamental woodland garden, home to exotic shrubs and trees, ponds and streams. Close to the start/finish of the route is King Henry VIII's Mound, the highest point within the park, from where there is a protected view of St Paul's Cathedral in the City of London over 10 miles to the east. You can enjoy this view, which has been present since 1710 from inside Pembroke Lodge gardens and makes a great finale to the walk.

Pembroke Lodge also has a well-stocked café with a lovely outdoor terrace as well as toilets and baby changing facilities. Snacks can also be purchased from the kiosk at Pen Ponds car park.

1. From the car park and with your back to Pembroke Lodge, take the path to your right past the refreshment kiosk. The path almost immediately splits – bear right away from the road and follow the fence of Pembroke Lodge's gardens. When the fence ends, turn right and head downhill on the track to the left of the steps which bears left down the hill. The track is bumpy and can be muddy. After 300 metres you reach the bottom of the hill and join the main path leftwards for a further 300 metres. The grassy field to your left is used for kite flying and you may see some adventurous types being pulled round the field on a kite buggy!

2. The path meets with the road at Ham Gate, where the pond presents your first opportunity to stop and feed the ducks. To continue the walk, cross the road and follow the Tasmin trail straight ahead for half a mile until you reach a further road crossing close to Kingston Gate. This well surfaced trail is flanked by beautiful oak trees, ferns, blackberry bushes and long grass.

3. Having crossed the road, head towards the car park entrance, cross the road again and head uphill on the grassy track that goes up between the trees. The path becomes very steep towards the top but the summit reveals a large flat area dotted with young oaks (and several benches for recovery). From the summit, take the grassy track to your left and after passing the fenced in circle of oaks (King's Clump) continue straight ahead – do not bear left towards the building in the distance. Gently descend through the trees and take the right

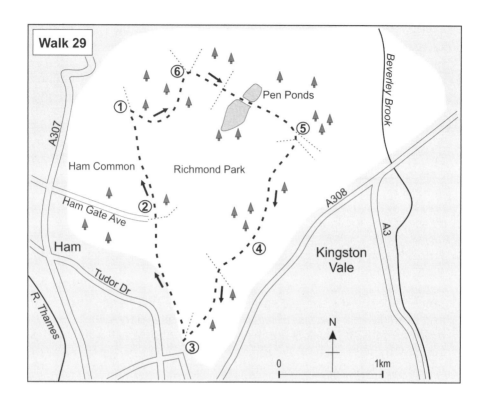

fork at the first junction you reach at the fenced in Dann's Pond. You will soon meet a second and third junction, both of which you should cross over to continue straight ahead. The path eventually brings you out at the Broomfield Hill entrance to the Isabella Plantation. A detour into the gardens is highly recommended.

4. From the gate of the plantation, follow the path with the fence to your left for the short distance until it splits – take the right fork. Cross the horse track and head downhill. At the bottom of the hill, cross the horse track again and continue straight ahead toward the car park in the distance.

5. From the car park, follow the signposts for the Capital Ring Walk towards Pen Ponds. The path cuts through the two ponds and heads

uphill. Having ascended three quarters of the hill, take the path to the left marked with the Capital Ring arrow. Take a moment to look back at the picturesque view of the ponds.

6. Continue to follow the Capital Ring arrows as you return to Pembroke Lodge, on the path that hugs the perimeter of the Queen Elizabeth's Plantation. The final road crossing back to the car park is a busy one so take care.

Walk 30
Wimbledon Common

Another walk in one of London's fine open spaces. You really feel more like you are in the countryside than the city in this oasis of tranquility in zone three of the capital. You will more than likely see horses out for a ride on many bridleways and plenty of ducks and swans at the beautiful Queensmere Pond.

The Common is good buggy walking terrain, making use of wide paths and cycleways and although there are several undulations, none are too challenging. Watch out for low flying golf balls as you will cross Wimbledon Common golf course at various points but signs warn you of the direction they'll be coming from and the golfers themselves are easily identifiable in their red uniform. A section of the route follows the Capital Ring Walk, a 75 mile circular walk through London's green spaces.

Distance	3 miles
Allow	2 hours
Map	OS 1:25000 Explorer 161. Grid reference TQ230725
Getting there	The walk starts from the Wimbledon Windmill car park, signposted from Wimbledon Parkside (A219). Parking is free. It is easily accessible by public transport, just take the train, tube or tram to Wimbledon Station and then jump on the 93 bus up Wimbledon Hill for the 5 minute ride to Parkside Hospital. Take the first left after disembarking for a short walk to the start of the route

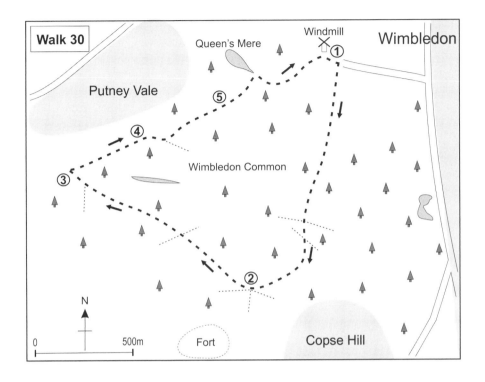

1. From the car park walk back in the direction of the road but take the first right through the green gate past the ranger's office. The ranger's horse will likely be grazing in the small paddock in front of the office. Follow the wide gravel track (known as Inner Windmill Road) with the golf course on your right for half a mile ignoring all intersecting bridleways and footpaths. The track then bears to the right and crosses the golf course.

2. Go through the white gate and fork left along the track which quickly meets a tarmac road. Continue right past Springwell Cottage to a small car park where there is a choice of two paths ahead. Ignore the right-hand track and continue straight ahead through another white gate and into woodland on the Robin Hood bridleway – though I would recommend using the cycleway that runs alongside the bridleway for an easier passage. Descend gently through the dense and beautiful woodland for ¾ mile.

3. At the crossroad at the bottom of the track turn right immediately before the bridge over Beverley Brook along the path marked 'No horses' which continues through a pretty wood alongside the brook.

4. When you reach an intersection with a tree in the centre, take the right-hand path marked 'No Cycling'. Shortly after take a more minor path to the left signposted for the 'Capital Ring Walk'. The remainder of the walk follows the well marked Capital Ring and makes going off track unlikely. Gently head up through the woods with playing fields through the trees on your left. Turn right at the next intersection and after a further 30 metres take the left hand fork. The hill's summit meets with the golf course and you should continue straight ahead until the path starts to drop back down again.

5. Where the track splits into 3, take the centre path (also marked with the Capital Ring signpost) and descend to Queensmere pond. The pond is a lovely spot and while you could head straight back to the car park,

Feeding the ducks at Queensmere pond

I would wholly recommend taking the short detour around the pond. Whichever option you choose, you will need to head right back uphill to return to the Windmill car park.

More books for intrepid pushchair walkers!

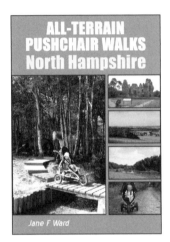

ALL-TERRAIN PUSHCHAIR WALKS: NORTH HAMPSHIRE

Jane F Ward

30 carefully selected all-terrain buggy walks in beautiful North Hampshire. From strolls through ancient forests, heathland rambles to spectacular uplands romps. Whether you're walking to keep fit or to enjoy the great outdoors.

£8.99

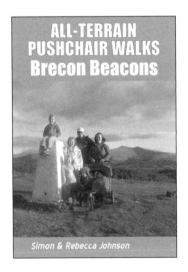

ALL-TERRAIN PUSHCHAIR WALKS: BRECON BEACONS

Simon & Rebecca Johnson

This book is written for families wanting to take their children walking using All Terrain Pushchairs (ATPs) on beautiful walks in the Brecon Beacons National Park. The 30 walks are also suitable for families without ATPs and anyone wishing to enjoy a walk without too much gradient and few if any stiles. The paths are suitable for double ATPs, as the authors have walked them all with their own children. Above all, get out into the wonderful, easily accessible Brecon Beacons, and enjoy the beauty, the nature and the tranquillity of this Welsh National Park.

£8.99

ALL-TERRAIN PUSHCHAIR WALKS: PEAK DISTRICT

Alison Southern

The Peak District, in the heart of the country, has some of England's most picturesque landscapes, from the White Peak in the south with its rocky outcrops and steep hills, to the Dark Peak in the north with peat moss moorland and stunning vistas. This book is for families with all-terrain pushchairs and buggies, and for everyone wishing to avoid as many stiles and obstacles as possible. Includes family-friendly attractions, trees to identify, birds and plants to spot, and lots more to discover. Have fun while you walk enjoying the amazing views, have some healthy exercise and spend time with the family away from the modern world.
£8.99

ALL-TERRAIN PUSHCHAIR WALKS: YORKSHIRE DALES

Rebecca Terry

Find out the best of what the Yorkshire Dales has to offer with these 30 tried and tested all-terrain pushchair walks through open moorland and country estates, and alongside the beautiful and dramatic rivers for which this National Park is renowned. The walks are all accurately graded and have at-a-glance symbols making choosing easier.
£8.99

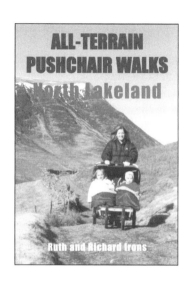

ALL-TERRAIN PUSHCHAIR WALKS: NORTH LAKELAND

Ruth & Richard Irons

Here are 30 walks across North Lakeland from Ennerdale Water to Lowther Park, Haweswater to Bassenthwaite. You'll find something to suit every type of walker – from Sunday Strollers to Peak Baggers and everyone else in between! Ruth and Richard Irons are experienced parents and qualified outdoor pursuits instructors – a reliable combination!
£8.99

ALL-TERRAIN PUSHCHAIR WALKS: SOUTH LAKELAND

Norman Buckley

"This book is fantastic – a perfect guide for parents" – Kathleen Jones (Lakeland Book of The Year Awards, 2005). Enjoy fabulous Lakeland scenery – north to south, from Grasmere to Grizedale Forest, and west to east, from Coniston to Kendal – you'll be spoilt for choice!
£8.99

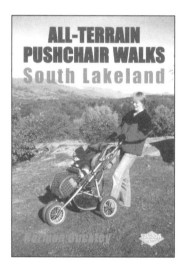

ALL-TERRAIN PUSHCHAIR WALKS: CHESHIRE

Norman Buckley

Enjoy these easy walks that range from the stunning peaks of East Cheshire to Mid-Cheshire's sandstone ridge, with the Cheshire plain in between. Amble along picturesque canal tow paths and disused railway lines or choose more adventurous walks through Macclesfield Forest. And as if that's not enough, there are visits to Cheshire's pretty villages, historic parklands and stately homes.
£8.99

ALL-TERRAIN PUSHCHAIR WALKS: SNOWDONIA
Zoë Sayer & Rebecca Terry
A superb collection of pushchair-friendly walks for North Wales. These 30 routes explore the spectacular scenery of the Snowdonia National Park – including an adventurous walk that takes you and a pushchair half-way up Snowdon! The walks range from simple riverside strolls to full-on alpine-style stomps.
£8.99

PUSHCHAIR PATHS: EAST MIDLANDS
Melanie Graham
This is the first pushchair-friendly walking book for the East Midlands written by enthusiastic walker, writer and 'East Midlander', Melanie Ramet. Melanie has written 25 'ORPing' (Off-Road Pushchairing) routes to encourage unrestricted access into the heart of the wonderful East Midlands countryside, where walkers can be confident there will be no unexpected obstacles to negotiate the pushchair over, under or through!
£8.99

Also available from Sigma

NEW FOREST WALKS
DISCOVERING THE PAST – A TIME TRAVELLERS GUIDE
Andrew Walmsley

Explore the New Forest with this series of 16 walks through ancient landscapes where long-forgotten bumps, hollows and moss-clad earthen banks have stories to tell of Bronze and Iron Age peoples, Romans, Normans and others who lived, worked and hunted here. Illustrated throughout with colour photographs.
£12.99

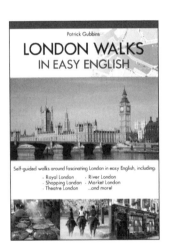

LONDON WALKS IN EASY ENGLISH
Patrick Gubbins

Forget the boring "walk books" that take you down quiet streets where nothing happens. *London Walks in Easy English* knows where the busy, exciting places in the capital are, and makes sure you see London life with all its colour, tradition, food, views, art, beautiful buildings and, most importantly, its sense of fun. What other book of walks takes you inside the classrooms of London University, into courtrooms to see real trials in progress, into shops to try exotic food, and to the big attractions but also to many other fascinating places that even Londoners don't know? *London Walks in Easy English* takes you through the capital's busiest and liveliest areas, with easy-to-follow walks in conversational-level English.
£9.99

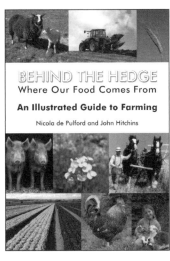

BEHIND THE HEDGE
Where Our Food Comes From
An Illustrated Guide to Farming
Nicola de Pulford & John Hithins

Behind the Hedge is for everyone who wants to know more about the food we eat, the land it is grown and reared on, and those who farm it. It is an easy-to-follow guide which will help you identify in their natural environment our crops, fruit and farm animals, agricultural buildings and machinery, the farming landscape and the wildlife it supports.

Never again will you mistake a field of wheat for one of barley, or an Aberdeen Angus cow for a Hereford. By dipping in and out of this beautifully illustrated book, you will learn to recognise the crops, farm animals and wildlife on the other side of the hedge.

£12.99

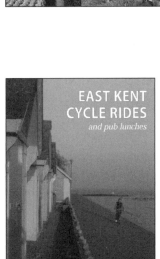

EAST KENT CYCLE RIDES
and pub lunches
Helen Thomson

Brief Description:From the flat open vistas of Romney Marsh to the steep sunken lanes of the North Downs East Kent offers cyclists a variety of terrain, and you're usually never far from a great pub. The rides in this guide take you through East Kent's sleepy backwaters avoiding major roads where at all possible. Most of the rides start at a railway station for ease of use for those who prefer to leave the car at home. The majority are circular tours and some incorporate sections of the national cycle route network. Designed for flexibility of use, many of the rides incorporate both shorter routes (core pedals) with suggestions for longer or more challenging runs (extended pedals) for the more energetic.

£8.99

WALKS ON THE SOUTH DOWNS
26 WALKS IN THE NEW NATIONAL PARK
Louise Schweitzer
Twenty five circular trails range from five to ten miles long around some of the most unspoilt and spectacular scenery in England on waymarked public footpaths, bridleways, old coach roads and an occasional tarmac lane. Most routes feature a particular landmark, viewpoint, monument or preserved antiquity, touching the more familiar long distance trails in passing, but creating new viewpoints for the present from some perspectives of the past.
£8.99

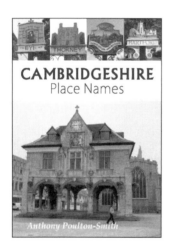

CAMBRIDGESHIRE PLACE NAMES
Anthony Paulton-Smith
Ever wondered why our towns and villages are named as they are? Who named them and why? Towns, villages, districts, hills, streams, woods, farms, fields, streets and even pubs are examined and explained. The definitions are supported by anecdotal evidence, bring to life the individuals and events which have influenced the places and the way these names have developed.This is not simply a dictionary but a history and will prove invaluable not only for those who live and work in the county but also visitors and tourists, historians and former inhabitants, indeed anyone with an interest in Cambridgeshire.
£8.99

All of our books are available through booksellers.
For a free catalogue, please contact:

**Sigma Leisure, Stobart House, Pontyclerc
Penybanc Road, Ammanford SA18 3HP
Tel: 01269 593100 Fax: 01269 596116**
info@sigmapress.co.uk   www.sigmapress.co.uk